SAVOURY MERINGUE
and other plays

James Saunders

AMBER LANE PRESS

All rights whatsoever in these plays are strictly reserved and application for professional performance, etc., should be made before rehearsal to:
Margaret Ramsay Ltd.,
14a Goodwin's Court,
St Martin's Lane,
London WC2N 4LL

Application for amateur performance should be made to:
Samuel French Ltd.,
26 Southampton Street,
London WC2E 7JE.

No performance may be given unless a licence has been obtained.

First published in 1980 by
Amber Lane Productions Ltd.,
Amber Lane Farmhouse ,
The Slack,
Ashover, Derbyshire S45 0EB.

Printed in Great Britain by
A. Wheaton & Co. Ltd., Exeter.

Typesetting and make-up by
Computerset (Phototypesetting) Ltd., Oxford.

Copyright © James Saunders, 1980

ISBN 0 906399 12 2

SAVOURY MERINGUE

For Audrey

Contents

Savoury Meringue   9

Who Was Hilary Maconochie?   29

Play for Yesterday   53

Birdsong   79

Poor Old Simon   105

SAVOURY MERINGUE

Characters

HESSIAN
JACK
FERDINAND
BODY

Savoury Meringue was first performed by the Ambiance Lunch-Hour Theatre Club at the Almost Free Theatre, London, on 14 April, 1971, with Prunella Scales as Hessian and Robert English as Jack. It was directed by Ed Berman.

Enter HESSIAN. *She carries the book with her, to which she may or may not refer at any time during any or all of her speeches.*

HESSIAN: The second time I said yes. By the way, I said, my name's Hessian. What's yours? You look a nice bit of stuff to me, he said. It's suggested I insult the audience. Your nose is too big. Oh fuck this. If your nose is too big you wouldn't have it, would you. Why should I insult you, you're nothing to me.

[*A clock chimes three.*]

Four o'clock. It's fast. The clock bit is fast. The chiming bit's slow as you've surmised. The clock itself bit says six. It's really eight. Twenty-two hours fast or thereabouts. Right, I want some help. Man has two eyes, two noses, two tits and two bellybuttons, true or false? False, except for twins. No, wait a minute.

[*She may whistle.*]

Would any gentleman care to come up? Any lady care to come down? If a maggot and a half ate an apple and a half in a day and a half. No, I got that wrong. And a quarter. If an apple and a half ate a maggot and a half in a day and a half and a quarter. How many . . . Here's my brother.

[*Enter* JACK.]

Tarpaulin. Jack Tarpaulin. Tarpaulin is thus his surname, which makes me Hessian Tarpaulin, not being married. How to slip in information about the characters. Why get married with a name like that and lose my only asset? It's not of course, my name's not Hessian Tarpaulin. I would've married a man called Rubberbacked Underlay only I couldn't find one. Fucking low music-hall, I ask you what have we come to. We call him Jack Tar for short, we don't of course. Whos we anyway? [*calling into the wings*] Whos we, whos we? He'll talk in a minute. When I've run out he'll carry on. I've run out. All right, bugger you too.

[*A dungeon door clangs shut.*]

Half past six.

JACK: What do you say to an inmate when you release him, outmate.

HESSIAN: Well done. We call him, no I told you that. Low fucking music-hall. Is this all we have left? Is it, is it, is it, is it. Low music fucking hall? Is this the end of the line? Low music ha-fucking-ll? Oh for the days of comedy of menace, theatre or whatever it was. Melo-bleeding-drama. The Bells. Shake — what was it? Might as well have the lions and the and the and be done with it. Throw the, to the. Thrown to the lions, why not. At least it had a beginning a middle and an end. There's going to be more than two of us I trust. I'll not keep my end up at this rate as the Bishop said at the sex marathon, oh God.

JACK: And how are you today, not so well thank God.

HESSIAN: Well done. Go have a look see if there's anyone else. As if I didn't know. This show lasts approximately thirty minutes. I have to draw your attention to the fact that the publicity for this show recommended you not to see it. There is also a notice outside to that effect. It's not on the programme only because by the time you read the programme you've made your decision. To invite you not to see a show you've already bought a ticket for would be hypocritical. Or not bought a ticket talking of critics. Say this three times quickly, no why should you.

JACK: No why should you no why should you no why should you.

HESSIAN: Brilliant. I have been asked to say that having come against our advice you are here under your own duress only. You are of course welcome to stay but should you wish to leave at any time please do so only have the decency to do it quietly. Then we'll see who our friends are. And relations. As to the apportioning of blame, if you are oldfashioned enough still to think in such terms, I have been asked to draw your attenttion to the fact that I'm doing it for the money. So is the director so is the author. So is the backstage staff and front of house. So is my brother, he's not my brother, and anyone else you may see. We are fulfilling our roles as you are. Only your not doing it for the money. I leave the conclusion to you. If you wish to leave, no I've said that, only don't expect a refund since the decision was yours in the first place. For our part, we expect as our due neither applause nor laughter any more than you should expect as your due that we should entertain you. We owe nothing to you, you owe nothing to us, I've been asked to stress that point. In short, we make fools of ourselves for cash, if you do it for nothing more fool you. I don't wish to be rude, I'm paid to say these lines. I don't necessarily agree with them though I may. My private views are my own business as yours are yours. In short, I've been requested to state that anyone creating a disturbance will be ejected, this is our place if you don't like it you know what you can do. Quietly. That's all I have to say. No offence. No, wait a minute. Yes. No, it's gone. I'll tell you later if I remember it.

[*Go to the wings, look out, come back.*]

Pause. I have been asked to state that at this point the author got fed up with it and went to bed with a Scotch — with a *Scotch*.

[*Pause.*]

JACK: What has three legs and a tail at the back, a three-legged elephant in retreat.

HESSIAN: Front.

JACK: What has three legs and a tail at the front, a three-legged elephant in retreat.

HESSIAN: What a good nights sleep will do. Oh for the unities of yesteryear. Where are they now where are they now. You don't look like my brother.

JACK: You got a brother?

HESSIAN: Feed line. Answer, no. Payoff.

JACK: Then how do you know I don't look like him?

HESSIAN: The humour derives from an ambiguity inherent in the statement, You don't look like my brother. One, you don't look like the man who is my brother, two, you don't look as I imagine my brother would look if I

had one, i.e. I can see no family resemblance, i.e. you
don't look like me. On the erroneous supposition that
my statement carried meaning one rather than
meaning two rests the joke. How easily we are amused.

JACK: A maggot a day keeps the apple away.

HESSIAN: That one's more difficult.

[*The phone rings.*]

Yes. Yes. Yes. I am to tell you that progress is slow. A
raw morning, foggy and waterlogged, typical November weather, not conducive to creative activity, rather
to hibernation. Many days nay weeks of torpor inter-
spersed with false starts gave reason for pessimism not
to say despair. However, and note the gleam of that
however which may be likened to the glimmer of light
glimpsed by a weary traveller, all is possibly after all
not lost. The present project, seen first as no more than
a floating straw, grows hour by hour to an ever more
sizeable lump of flotsam, and still floats, still bears
weight. From inauspicious beginnings who knows
what may not grow. A floating turd is as good as a
luxury liner to a drowning man, be it large enough.
Better, easier to get hold of. All one asks is to keep ones
head above water. Moreover and consider that moreover, a second light flickers on the horizon, moreover it
is not impossible, nay even confidently expected that
. . .

[*Refers to phone.*]

Yes. That the very formlessness of the present project
may in some way provide in some way both the
freedom allowing true organic growth . . .

[*The phone rings.*]

Yes. As humus to a tree; and, paradoxically, also a
matrix by which, within which, that growth will be
defined.

[*The phone rings.*]

As a seed. Big deal. Further bulletins will not
necessarily be issued.

[*The phone rings.*]

Yes. I am to conclude with a rhetorical question for

consumption off the premises. What is it that drives us on.

JACK: Come here.

> [HESSIAN *goes to him. Stand looking at him for some time. Then he hits her.*]

Say your sorry.

HESSIAN: Get fucked.

> [*Stand looking at one another for some time.*]

All right, I'm sorry.

> [*He hits her. Stand looking at one another for some time. He hits her.*]

Charming. Oh I'm tired. I'm not really. If we had a few things about we could . . . If we. Listen. Given — no. Yes, given that we have here a world of infinite possibilities why are they not realised?

> [*The phone rings. Lift it, put it straight down again.*]

Look at it this way, within these magic confines anything is possible. Anyone may enter, any thing or combination of things known or invented for the purpose may be thrust into view to be used according to ones fancy. One can provide characters up to any number consistent with the physical dimensions who may singly or in chorus in any combination or series of combinations open their traps and partaking of the myriad complexities of our marvellous language say whatever the hell they like to each other without let, hindrance or fear of imprisonment.

> [*At 'fancy' the phone rings. Treat it as before, only without stopping talking.*]

Lights sounds Peppers Ghost back projection front projection nudity and song. Well then.

> [*The phone rings. Let it, then pick it up and listen.*]

Hard luck. That's *your* job mate. Fuck you too.

> [*Put it down.*]

Bloody liberty. Come that language with me. I hope for the worst, that's all, I hope for the worst.

> [*Music: Fascination — Harry James.*]

Well that's something.

[*Sing to it.*]

Peace offering no doubt.

> [*Sing, dance.* JACK *also dances. Both dance as if with a partner, but separately. You happen to be facing one another when the music suddenly stops in midbar. Look at one another for some time. He hits her.*]

Charming.

> [*Music: Goodnight Sweetheart — Mantovani and his Singing Strings.*]

Shut that racket!

> [*The music stops. Pause.*]

It won't last the night.

> [FERDINAND *shoots onstage as if propelled from behind. Look about in panic for a moment, scutter off again. Appear again as before, scutter off the other side.* HESSIAN *picks up the phone with a decisive gesture. Listen, shake it, put it down again.*]

Humus my arse.

> [*Pause.* FERDINAND *comes in as before, tries to scutter off as before. But a dungeon door clangs shut. Scutter off the other way. A dungeon door clangs shut. Sit in a corner, huddled as small as possible.*]

Draconian measures. Ferdinand. We call him Ferd for short because he's the fird and he's short.

JACK: A Ferdinand is worth two in the bush.

HESSIAN: We're really breaking new ground.

> [*Go and stand by* FERDINAND, *waiting for him to do something. Nothing.*]

Ferd. Come forth.

> [*The phone rings.*]

Yes.

> [*Take it to* FERDINAND.]

It's for you.

> [*No response. Try to wedge it against his ear. Give up and hold it there.*]

Cry out when you finished.

> [*Stand there a while. Take it away to listen.*
> *Still going on, put it back. Stand there a while.*
> *Take it away and listen. Stopped. Put it down.*
> *Wait. Nothing.*]

Have a good talk did you? Something you got to do,
yes? Like to tell us all about it? Let us into the secret?
This is a hard nut, this one. Nothing to be afraid of you
know. All friends here. Like fuck we are. We're all set
on this old world together that's the way I look at it,
might as well make the best of it, rub along together as
best we can. Spread a little sunshine. Help to lighten
the other fellows load. Leave a little something to be remembered by and I don't mean a turd in a dark corner.
Flogging a dead horse. Help me get him to his feet.

> [*Ignore her.*]

It's not so bad you know. Out here. It's worse inside.
Come out. Try it. I'll kick the buggers head in in a
minute. You are needed you know. We're all needed.
We all have our place in the scheme of things. Somewhere out there the master mariner has his hand on the
helm, keeping his eyes on the far horizon, he knows
where we're going. Big symbolic bit, what about an
extract or two from the Dover Road. Come along old
chap. You prick. Get your. It's no good is it. We all got
to pull on the ropes you know. Many hands make light
work. A shit pie shared is a shit pie halved. Why
should I do it all you lazy sod. Poor love look at him.
Get up you bugger. Help me get him up.

> [*Bend to grasp his arm.* JACK, *behind you,*
> *takes a run up and a leap and lands on your*
> *back, piggyback fashion. Say nothing. Your*
> *hands go automatically to hold his legs, stag-*
> *ger forward a bit naturally. Finish standing,*
> *just, a bit crouched, waiting for it to go away. It*
> *doesn't. Let go his legs. No good, he has them*
> *tight round your waist and his arms round*
> *your neck. Fall slowly to your knees then onto*
> *your hands. He lets go with his hands as you do*

*so, and is sitting you like a horse. Put your head
up, try to look round. Go back to a crouching
position, all good exercise, while he grabs
round your neck again, then you topple over
backwards till you are on top of him. From
there you'll probably both roll sideways to face
the audience. Stay there a while.*]

If that's the way you want it.

[*Stay there, resigned, assuming something will
happen.*]

Let's have some music, shall we?

[*No music.*]

A zombie a sadist and me.

[*The phone rings. After a while it stops.*]

I'm laughing. Get yourself out of this one, you sod.

[*The phone rings. After a while it stops.*]

It's out of my hands. I'm laughing.

[*Make a sudden struggle to escape. Useless.
Relax again.*]

Laughing. Stop that. Listen. Whatever your name is. I
think we've started off on the wrong foot with each
other. Will you stop that. I'm willing to accept the
possibility that you've got the idea we're not ideally
suited. Is that the case, have I hit the nail on the head? If
so I'm very sorry but I don't — *don't* — don't think
your behaviour so far is likely to do anything but
aggravate a situation which at best will always be
strained. I'd like to make a suggestion, are you
listening? I'd like to suggest we bear in mind that we're
a couple of civilised human beings and behave accor-
dingly. Turn it up. We're stuck with each other so we'll
have to make the best of a bad job. And that goes for see
no evil over there too. In short, oh it's pitiful, might as
well talk to a brick wall. I've been in some un-
theatrical situations in my time but this beats cock-
fighting, will you leave that off you dirty devil!

[*A groan from* FERDINAND.]

I'll tell you something, if I ever get loose I'm kicking
your head in for a start. Oh well I could be buried up to

me neck I spose. [*loudly*] I notice the phone's stopped ringing. You'll grasp the significance of that I trust, you two. We been abandoned, cut loose. We're adrift in the open sea on a turd without a rudder. For which I may add you can thank yourselves. Well done. One thing's certain, I did my bit, I kept my end up. That I near ruptured myself doing it's neither here nor there, who gives a shit, not you two that's obvious, I could've saved myself the effort. But there you are it's the same all over it's not new to me. A sense of responsibility to oneself and ones fellow creatures is a standing invitation to a spit in the eye. These days duty's a four letter word. Don't think I'm surprised, I've had it all my life, from personal relations upwards. It runs right through. Give 'em an inch and your buggered, I've come to expect it as my due. Oh I could tell you a thing or two. Why should I. Find out for yourselves. Forget it. Put me down as a born victim, don't let it worry you. I can't help trying, my mother was frightened by a romantic idealist, hard cheese, forget it.

> [*Look round as best you can, and see* FERDINAND. *He's cautiously unrolled himself and stood up, crept across to you and is stood staring at the two of you.*]

Come in it's lovely.

> [*Panic, he scuttles back to his place.*]

You can't say a thing can you. Diplomacy was never my strong suit. Should've grabbed his ankle. Ferd. Ferdinand. Or whoever you are. Listen. This is important. Can you hear me? Nod your head if you can hear me. Are you nodding your head? Well anyway, listen. You think I'm angry with you don't you? Well I'm not. Not even slightly disillusioned, do you believe me? I only want to help you. I think you need help. You have a slight hangup don't you? You can tell me I'm yore friend we are friends aren't we Ferd, Ferdinand, I'd like to be yore friend would you like to be mi friend shall we be friends lets eh? You don't want to be ashamed of your hangup Ferd we all got hangups, whats a kink between friends. No I don't mean kink, your not kinky are you, course your not, querk I meant. I'll tell you a secret Ferd, I got querks'd make your hair stand on end, doesn't bother me though, I'm broadminded, we've all got our funny ways join the club mate. Ferd? Are you there? There better out than in you know. Tisn't the hangup does the damage it's the hiding it away, all the doctors tell you that, spect they have already haven't they? Ferd. It's like holding back your wind. We all get wind so why rupture yourself. Nature will out. What's a kink but a psychological fart? My guess is, Ferdy, your repelled by the human form, right or wrong? Tell you what, Ferdy, you come over here and we'll have a good old chinwag about our hangups, you tell me your querks and then I'll tell you my querks, how'd you like that eh?

[*Pause.*]

Drop dead then you bent bugger.

[*The phone rings.*]

Answer the telephone Ferdy.

[*He doesn't ov coarse.*]

Ferdy it could be important. Fuck could be it *is* important. Answer the phone you bugger before it —!

[*The phone stops.*]

Ferdinand, you just forfeited my sympathy. Crouch there then. Starve to death with the rest of us. This is stalemate mate.

> [*The phone rings. Sudden frantic squirm to get out of* TARPAULIN's *clutches. No resistance, your out of his arms. Look round in surprise. He's asleep. Suddenly remember the phone which is still ringing. Make a dive for it. It stops, as your hand gets to it. Give it a couple of seconds, then pick it up, without much hope, put it to your ear, put it down again. Stand up if not up already. Look round at* FERD, *at* TARPAULIN, *at the audience in outrage.*]

So.

> [*Go over to* FERDINAND, *stand over him,*

think about kicking his head in. FERDY
*scrounches up even smaller. Leave him, pick
up the phone, nothing. Go to wings, look out,
nothing. Come back, look at* JACK, *wonder
about giving him a shake, go decisively to the
phone, pick it up, bang the jigger up and
down. Slam the phone down.*]

Right. Now we know where we stand.

*[Defiant statement. Then start to realise the
implications. Telephone. Make a dash for it,
pick it up and listen.]*

Latest bulletin: Following a satisfactory blastoff and
the successful if delayed firing of stage two all systems
were assumed to be at go go go. This assumption is
now felt to have erred on the side of the overly optimis-
tic. Stage three has failed to ignite. In short, a degree of
apprehension has been evinced as to the completion of
the project. To put it plainly.

[The phone rings. Take it, listen, put it down.]

One finger is on the destruct button. No wait.

[Pick up the phone.]

Listen —

[Shrug, phone down.]

In a word, another cockup.

*[The phone rings. Take it, speak im-
mediately.]*

No listen, you can't — However what? What? Do
what? Me do what? You must be joking. Sorry wrong
number. Try the Palladium.

*[Slam phone down. Change your mind, pick it
up.]*

No wait a minute . . .

[Too late. Phone down.]

Sheer irresponsibloodybility. Oh I get the message.
The bell's rung never fear. I've had it before it's the
story of my life. Moral blackmail. You won't catch me
on that jag again. Two can play at that game. However
. . . Oh, fuck that.

[Lie down on your back and close your eyes.]

Put upon I may be from the age of birth but at least I can fight it.

> [*Pause. A squeaking noise as of unoiled pulleys. Open your eyes, stare upwards. The squeaking stops, close your eyes again.* FERDINAND *has uncoiled enough to stare at* HESSIAN's *prone form with one eye. He gets to the kneeling position cautiously, but the phone rings as he starts to crawl towards her. Freeze. The phone rings a while then stops. After a safe period he starts to crawl again but stops as* HESSIAN *opens her eyes and speaks.*]

Think I ought to jump into the breach then? Pull the cat out of the fire? Turn disaster into triumph through sheer force of personality, talent and my indomitable will? Get up and make you cry shall I? Get you in stitches with my inimitable wit? Like my life story with it, sure why not. I'll throw in a song and dance while I'm at it, why not, then strip off in case your attentions flagging and a quick fuck with any gentle-man in the front row. Why not? Except I'm not going to. Do it your bloody selves. Be thyself and thyself alone, that's my motto.

> [See FERD.]

Perseverence.

> [*Close your eyes. Squeak. Open eyes, look up. Squeak stops. Close your eyes. Pause.*]

I had this bloke. No what business is it of yours.

> [*Pause. Up on your elbow to tell your tale.*]

Six years, six years I had him round my neck. His name was Albert Ross believe it or not, well it should have been. He got the moral blackmail off to a fine art. Pulled me down into the shit like a grand master. He was paranoid. He'd lost a foot. He was impotent. He got boils. He got dandruff till he was cured by going bald. He was a right mess he should've been put down only no-one ever had the heart. Look at me he said. Look at my background. Look at my upbringing. Look at my hangups. Look at my boils. I'm dis-gusting I know that. You can't live with me, no-one can live with me, and keep their dinner down. I'm a cruel filthy thoughtless disgusting tyke and I'll drag you under. Leave me, I'm not worth it, I'll get by till I go rotten enough to die. The bastard. Took him six years to drag me under and I don't think he was trying all that hard. The only promise he ever kept. He reduced me to a heap of quivering human debris and he never stopped apologising till I went into the nursing home. The end of a beautiful relationship. He couldn't visit me of course, it was too painful for him, knowing he'd put me there. I finally got home there was a note on the mantelpiece, where else. Written on toilet paper if you'll believe me. He couldn't live with what he'd done to me so he'd gone off with a mutual friend. Took his boot his whips his spurs the lot, never again. It's all completely untrue of course, needless to say. I'm a happily married woman, his name's Ted and we've got two lovely kiddies a boy and a girl, that's a lie too, I'm not married, I'm just an actress on a stage and I'm sick of it, I'm not really.

[*Down on your back again, whoever you are, close your eyes. Squeak. Open them, look up.* FERD *freezes again. Close your eyes.* JACK *stirs, stretches, yawns, gets up and eyes* HESSIAN *for a while. Her eyes open, she watches you till you wander off to the back of the stage assuming the stage has got a back to it if not your on your own mate. Then close them again. Fire bucket hanging back of stage. Stand facing it. Pause.* FERDY *has crawled closer, but only while no-one else was doing anything. Piddling sound in the fire bucket.* FERDY *has crawled right up to* HESSIAN *and is suddenly on her, making as if to return to the womb head first, emitting obscure noises. Try to get him off, outraged, but he clings like a dose of crabs. Struggle till you finally manage to break free and stand up panting.* FERDY *curls up into a ball. Stand looking down at him.*]

I pity you I really do.

> [*Squeaking noise. Look up.* JACK, *finished piddling, takes a run up and lands on your back as before. You stagger forward under the impetus, trip over* FERDY *and end up on the floor, which is a good thing because it dislodges* JACK *so you can get up quickly before he has a chance to grab you again, so avoiding a boring repetition.* JACK *gets up, brushes down his leopardskin jockstrap, strikes a pose and flexes his muscles.* FERDY *is all crunched up again.*]

You couple of turds.

> [*Pick up the phone.*]

Is this the —

> [*Put it down again.*]

Is this the best you can do? Is this the limit of your inventiveness, my God!

JACK: A Terdinand is worth two in the bush.

> [JACK *stands flexing his muscles and striking poses.* FERDY *sits now with his head in his hands. Pause. Squeaking noise. The thing finally descends from the flies. A body, on a tabletop, all done up in bandages Komic Kuts fashion, one leg up in the air. Face covered except a hole for the mouth. If there aren't any flies it can be pulled on on a tea trolley or use your inventiveness.* HESSIAN *stands looking at it. Pause. The phone rings. Pause. Take it. Listen. Shake it. Nothing.*]

JACK: He's shot his bolt.

> [HESSIAN *turns to stare at him. Then at the* BODY. *An obscure noise from* FERDY. *Give him a look too. Back to* BODY. *Go to the phone, wait for it to ring, one hand ready. It doesn't. Look front. Open your mouth to say something. Nothing to say.* JACK *is now doing the occasional knees bend, nothing energetic, more for show, almost slow motion.*]

HESSIAN: He's what?

[*No answer. Go to* BODY, *take a look at it.*]

BODY: Help.

HESSIAN: What?

BODY: Help.

HESSIAN: Your joking. [*to the audience*] Let me say one thing however. Fuck the however, let me say one thing. I want no sympathy from anyone. If your feeling sorry for me your casting your seed on barren ground. I'm tough mate. I may not be old but I'm experienced, wrap up you self-centred cow, can't you see I'm in the middle of a speech?

[*This to the* BODY *which has thrown in another 'Help'.*]

Yes I've sampled the wares of this cheapjack line of bankrupt stock they call, I forget what they do call it now. What was I talking about?

FERDY: Groan.

HESSIAN: Don't call me a philanthropist, I don't mean philanthropist. Don't call me a —

[*The phone rings.*]

Fuck off!

[*The phone stops.*]

Don't call me a, where was I. Listen, I've had enough of this, let's get to the point. I know what your waiting for, never fear, not to meet me at the stage door that's for sure. Message is what you want, right, have I scored a bullseye? I have learnt one or two items in my life, I didn't spend it lolling on a bed of honey and roses, I was born and bred in Shit Street mate. Right, hang on to your knickers, here comes the message. However —

[*The phone rings. Take it.*]

Yes! What? Abort, what's abort? Look mate — Look mate, all you've done for me so far is fuck me up. What kind of a prick do you think I am? I relied on you. I had faith in you. And what did I get? A sadist, a masochist and an Egyptian mummy that's been run over by a pyramid. I'm an optimist, mate, but not after it starts hurting. I waited for you to help me out of the shit and what did I get? Bugger all. And now, just when I've

realised I'm not getting any help from any bastard but
number one, just when I start getting a good run up for
a single-handed flying finish to this load of old crap,
you cut the thread with this abort abort. Stick your
abort mate. What? I don't give a. I don't give a shit if its
meaningful or meaning*less*, I'm a pro mate. I'm a professional, when I take on a task I finish it, meaningful
schmeaningful, and I don't give a squirrels anus for
your integrity neither. I don't think you've got the
message. I don't need you. I don't want to be rude but
heres my suggestion. Stick your meaningfulness up
your arse; and then stick your integrity up your arse;
and then piss off, and take your abort with you. And let
me finish.

    [*Slam the phone down. It starts ringing again.*
    Throw the whole lot offstage. Pause.]

Bloody liberty . . . Where the fuck was I.

BODY: Help.

    [*Got to the* BODY, *glare at it.*]

HESSIAN: Do you want your foot twisted?

    [*Turn to* JACK.]

What's abort anyway? What's this abort?

    [*Turn back.*]

Now I lost the swing of it. I had it there, I had it, I was
all set to finish this off with a flourish and retire with
dignity if not with grace, and no help from anyone.
Don't call me a misanthrope, call me a realist. Call me
what the fuck you like, makes no difference to me, it's
all words. If I keep on talking for long enough something'll come out of it. I had an important — not
important. I had something lined up to say, forgotten
what it was now. Would've rounded it off nicely I
know that, I got it just before the phone went, now I
lost it. Would've given it a kind of — [*Shape it with*
your hands.] You know. Would've made it seem sort
of. Very important, endings. I'm a pro, mate. Well,
never mind. Do the dying fall bit, eh? Waft out on a
minor key. Not what I hoped. But better than having it
off with a porcupine. [*to* BODY] Sorry love. No offence.

[*Pat its plaster.*]
[*to* JACK] Sorry mate. Some other time, eh?
[*Shake his hand, while he does exercises. Go to*
FERDY. *Pat his head.*]
If the lights went down now it wouldn't be too bad . . .
[*Pause.*] It was only an idea.
[*Lights.*]

THE END

WHO WAS HILARY MACONOCHIE?

Characters

Who Was Hilary Maconochie? was first performed at the Questors Theatre, Ealing, in June 1963, with the following cast:

MRS BRUTE	Doreen Ingram
MRS DRUDGE	Alex Mikellatos
HILDA	Sandra Turner

It was directed by John Miles Brown.

The first professional production was by the Theatre In The Round Company in Scarborough in 1963, with the following cast:

MRS BRUTE	Sheila Connor
MRS DRUDGE	Caroline Hunt
HILDA	Latilla Woodburn

It was directed by Arnold Beck.

A drawing room in the English style. MRS BRUTE
sits at her bureau making up her diary.

MRS BRUTE: Friday the nineteenth of October, 1972. In the
drawing room of a respectable detached house in
the Edwardian style, set in a quiet avenue of plane
trees one minute from Streatham Common, South
London, England, Mrs Mabel Brute, widow, sits
at her bureau making up her diary. "Friday the
nineteenth of October, 1972," she writes. "This
morning, on going as usual into the garden to
leave bread for the birds on the birdbath, one slice
of white and two of Hovis, I discovered that the
knuckle of bacon which I had hung from a tree for
the blue-tits had vanished. Since no tit of any kind
could carry off a complete knuckle, I suspect a
marauding cat, one of the thousands which roam
all night the streets and gardens of Streatham,
England. A lover of cats *and* of birds, my loyalty is
divided. Should I now hang another knuckle?
Much as I love cats, a knuckle a day is more than I
had in mind, besides which if the tits can get at the
knuckle and the cats can get at the knuckle the cats
can get at the tits, since God in his wisdom has so
fashioned cats as to love birds only in the gastro-
nomical sense. *This* is the dilemma in which I
find myself. Added to this, last night, following a
dream in which, left behind by an Antarctic Ex-
pedition, I paddled frantically across the South-
ern Ocean on an upturned canoe pursued by two
walruses together with the carpenter who came
last week to mend the rustic seat in the garden —
(an interesting association of ideas) — I awoke
suddenly to find that my hot-water bottle, now
cold, was leaking uncontrollably, and dripping
onto the linoleum. I was given this bottle by my
late husband the week after our honeymoon; it
was of the best Empire rubber and had a flannel
cover done in the Macdonald tartan, in honour of

Mr Ramsay Macdonald who was then Prime Minister. I feel a sense of personal loss. The barometer today stands at twenty-five and a half inches . . .

[*Meanwhile* HILDA *the maid has come in.*]

HILDA: A word with regard to the late husband, Roger Brute, sandy-haired, sandy-moustached, blue-pinstriped Monday to Friday, Salt-and-pepper plusfours Saturday to Sunday, outdoor game golf, indoor game bridge, hobby the growing of prize vegetable marrows, religion Conservative, politics Church of England, average daily consumption of toilet tissue not counting Christmas and Bank Holidays, 3.72 sheets. Favourite meal brown windsor soup followed by boiled mutton with Yorkshire pudding, dumplings, boiled potatoes, boiled cabbage and boiled vegetable marrow garnished with Oxo cubes, followed by Christmas pudding and custard. Died 1932 of an exploded hot-water bottle: politics now unknown, religion unknown, hobbies nil, daily consumption of boiled mutton and toilet tissue, nil.

MRS BRUTE: One thing troubles me —

HILDA: — writes Mrs Brute.

MRS BRUTE: — and that is this: glancing through the column of *The Times* headed *In Memoriam* I came across the following: "Hilary Maconochie. In evergreen memory of a dear friend, the solace of my widowhood, passed away the nineteenth of October 1933, of an exploded hot-water bottle. From Mabel Brute. *Volens et valens. Semper paratus. Suaviter in modo, fortiter in re. Rara avis in terris.*" On telephoning the *Times* office I was informed that this self-same paragraph has appeared every year since 1934 and will continue to appear until the end of time, or *The Times,* whichever comes first, paid for by a trust fund set up by this same Mabel Brute. The question is this: am *I* the Mabel Brute, widow, referred to? *Suaviter in modo, fortiter in re?* Who the devil was Hilary Maconochie?

HILDA: So she muses, as well she may.
           [HILDA *goes out, and comes quickly in
           again.*]
           Enter the maid Hilda. You rang, madam?
MRS BRUTE: No.
HILDA: Exit the maid.
           [*She goes out.* MRS BRUTE *rings.* HILDA
           comes in.]
           You —?
MRS BRUTE: Hilda.
HILDA: Madam.
MRS BRUTE: Where does the barometer stand now?
HILDA: In the hall, madam.
MRS BRUTE: I see. Hilda —
HILDA: Madam.
MRS BRUTE: Today is Friday.
HILDA: Madam.
MRS BRUTE: And the time?
HILDA: On the wall, madam.
MRS BRUTE: You misunderstand me, Hilda. I'm not asking
           where the clock *is,* but what the clock *says.*
           [*The clock chimes once, the half hour.*]
HILDA: Bong, madam.
MRS BRUTE: Very well. You may go.
HILDA: Go where, madam?
           [*Pause.*]
           What it is to be English ...
           [*Pause.*]
MRS BRUTE: The Isle of Man.
HILDA: Very good, madam.
           [*She is on her way out.*]
MRS BRUTE: Oh, Hilda ...
HILDA: Madam.
MRS BRUTE: Supposing — supposing I were to say a name to
           you. Would it mean anything to you?
HILDA: Which name?
MRS BRUTE: I'm not in the habit of discussing my affairs with
           the servants.
HILDA: I'm sorry, madam.
           [*She is going out.*]

MRS BRUTE: Let us say, for the sake of argument ... Hilary Maconochie.

[HILDA *turns and looks at her.*]

Well?

HILDA: I wish to give notice.

MRS BRUTE: It doesn't matter. You may go.

HILDA: Wh—?

MRS BRUTE: In the general sense.

[HILDA *goes out.* MRS BRUTE *looks at the clock, which has no hour hand.*]

But half past what?

[*Pause.*]

As I see it, there are six possibilities, all equally fantastic.

[*She counts on her fingers.*]

One: there exist two Mabel Brutes, widow. Two: such was the shock at meeting Hilary Maconochie for the first time that I lost my memory and have been in a state of amnesia ever since. Three: the knuckle bone was taken by a tawny owl in mistake for a rat. This poses a further question: if I replace the bone, and cat, tit and owl converge on it, what will the result be? Will the tit eat the bone while the owl eats the cat, will the owl eat the tit while the cat eats the bone, or will the tit eat the cat while the bone eats the owl? Or is there a fifth party involved? Four: *The Times* proper went out of circulation in 1933, and this mock edition has been kept running ever since by a person or persons unknown, merely in order to perpetuate this extraordinary practical joke at my expense. Five: since both my late husband and this Maconochie met their deaths by the same means, it's possible that they in fact knew one another, that Maconochie *gave* my late husband his hot-water bottle, set to explode in 1932, and afterwards took his own life by the same means. And that to make doubly sure he gave my late husband not one bottle but *two*, one of which my late husband gave me: and that luckily mine misfired,

and went off cold thirty years later. This is borne
out by the fact that the tartan on the bottle is not
Maconochie but *Macdonald*. A disguise. Six: —

> [*She realises the discrepancy, and looks
> down at her hand.*]

That Hilary Maconochie doesn't in fact exist. And
as a logical consequence, *The Times* doesn't exist,
my late husband doesn't exist, I don't exist, that
clock doesn't exist, my six fingers don't exist, this
bureau doesn't exist, the stage doesn't exist, the
theatre doesn't exist, the audience doesn't exist,
this bell doesn't exist —

> [HILDA *comes in.*]

HILDA: You rang, madam?

MRS BRUTE: Hilda ...

HILDA: Madam.

MRS BRUTE: Today being Friday, and the time half-past, I shall
be expecting Mrs Drudge to tea as usual. She'll be
here any minute; or in an hour's time, two hour's
time or so on.

HILDA: Shall I put out the card table then?

MRS BRUTE: Yes, yes, as usual.

> [HILDA *brings out a folding card table and
> sets it up. She finds cards and cribbage
> board and puts these on a table.*]

HILDA: Oh — is it to be cribbage? Or strip poker?

MRS BRUTE: Which did we play last week?

HILDA: Strip cribbage.

MRS BRUTE: Well, put it all out and we'll see what the tem-
perature's like. I really think strip poker's a sum-
mer game ... Hilda ...

HILDA: Madam.

MRS BRUTE: Buy three knuckle bones tomorrow.

HILDA: Human or animal, madam?

MRS BRUTE: See what's in the shops. And Hilda ... Regarding
... the person Maconochie ...

> [HILDA *averts her head violently.*]

Supposing for the sake of argument I were to ask
you whether — Have you strained your neck?

HILDA: I don't wish to speak of him, madam.

MRS BRUTE: But supposing for the sake of argument . . .

HILDA: I realise of course that I'm a prisoner in your employ. I'm bound to serve you, and that goes without saying, since I'm beholden to you for the very money I earn and the very bread I eat. It's absolutely out of the question that I should in any way deviate from absolute obedience and servitude which is the only birthright of those such as I who are fortunate enough to be born into such a servile and lowly station that not only are we free of the duty imposed upon those such as you to hand out your wealth, won by your ancestors at the cost of so much hell-fire, to those such as I in exchange for nothing but the miserable sweat of our brows and the lifeblood of our bodies, but are able because of the unfair advantage given us by our birth and upbringing actually to exchange our useless sweat and disgusting lifeblood for that which is set above thrones and princes, above popes and bishops, namely money.

MRS BRUTE: Yes, but supposing for the sake of argument . . .

HILDA: God forbid that I should say to you, madam, "Consider *yourself* as a humble serving-maid, dragging out her days in miserable servitude, her childhood fled, her youth sped by, her middle years fast approaching only to pass and be forgotten like all the rest, as the silent countryside speeds unrecognised and unacknowledged past the windows of a night express thundering inexorably to its final destination".

MRS BRUTE: With regard to the person Maconochie . . .

HILDA: Only to be confronted, when listless and beaten she has at last reconciled herself to her lot, by that hideous name . . . oh . . .

MRS BRUTE: Maconochie . . .?

HILDA: At the syllables of which the floodgates of memory burst open and all is remembered again as if it had never stopped happening, all, all, as if the events still lapped about her like the rising tide of some disgusting fluid which sucks at her ankles, oozes round her knees, rising higher and ever higher as she stands helplessly trapped in the quicksands of desire, lust and every imaginable vice, cut off from help by the rocks of her environmental situation, until all is engulfed, all besmirched, all washed away by the hideous neap-tide of carnality.

[*Pause.*]

MRS BRUTE: Go on.

HILDA: Can you imagine the poor serving wench, innocent as she then was, trusting, as only the innocent can trust, the smooth, courteous elder son of whom who could believe the worst, fresh as he was from Eton, the well-known English public school? What horror, then, as gentlemanly assistance of the forearm when the poor child stumbled with a tray of tea, merged imperceptibly into the casual friendly hand lightly touching the small of the back, the arm as though unconsciously round the waist while pausing to pass the time of day, the requests for sun-tan lotion at eleven o'clock on a winter's evening, shaving water at midnight, a hot-water bottle at two p.m. And then, under the threat of exposure to the father, to be passed on like a commodity to the younger son, not yet even *at* Eton, from thence, discovered by the father, to the father, under the threat of exposure to the mother — and from him to the friend of the family, the —oh, God — arch-fiend of all . . .

MRS BRUTE: *You?*

HILDA: Me — *what,* madam?

MRS BRUTE: Maconochie?

HILDA: Who?

[*The doorbell rings.*]

MRS BRUTE: Hilary Maconochie.

HILDA: Doorbell, madam.

MRS BRUTE: But — I had no sons at Eton. I had daughters at *Roedean.*

HILDA: Ha — so they deceived you too.

MRS BRUTE: But —

HILDA: Doorbell madam.

MRS BRUTE: Hilary —

HILDA: All has gone blank.

[*She makes for the door.*]

MRS BRUTE: It must be half past *four*. Make a note of it Hilda.

HILDA: Yes, madam.

[*She stops at the clock as she passes to pencil in the hour hand at half past four. The doorbell rings again.* HILDA *goes out.*]

MRS BRUTE: There is a pause. Mellowed by the recollections stirred by the foregoing, Mrs Mabel Brute, widow, sinks into an English aristocratic reverie, musing on that which has made England great and is now passing irrevocably away — boiled mutton with boiled potatoes, farthings, the crenellated towers of ancient insurance offices, railway trains, medieval hangings, and floggings, and New Zealand cheese ... "Where will it all end?" she says to herself, echoing unconsciously what her mother had said before her, and her grandmother and her great grandmother, and her great-great grandmother, and her great-great-great ...

[HILDA *appears at the door.*]

HILDA: Mrs Drudge, widow, madam.

MRS BRUTE: We shall have tea.

HILDA: Yes, madam.

[*She goes out.*]

MRS DRUDGE: Mrs Brute.

MRS BRUTE: Mrs Drudge. This *is* an expected surprise.

MRS DRUDGE: I'm sorry to be late.

MRS BRUTE: [*looking at the clock*] Are you late?

MRS DRUDGE: It's half past six, Mrs Brute. Past sunset. It's quite dark outside.

[*The daylight outside the french-windows-overlooking-the-lawn is suddenly switched off.*]

MRS BRUTE: Do you have such a thing as an india rubber?

[MRS DRUDGE *empties her handbag on to*

> *the table — powder compact, handker-*
> *chief, handcuffs, purse, model of the Eiffel*
> *Tower, pocket diary, saucer, cup, length*
> *of ribbon with, at the eventual end of it, a*
> *Union Jack.*]

MRS DRUDGE: I seem to have left it at home.

MRS BRUTE: It doesn't matter.

> [*She turns on the lamp and closes the cur-*
> *tains.*]

If you'll be so good as to tell me when it's twenty to seven.

MRS DRUDGE: Certainly. As a matter of fact I've been kept by the vicar.

MRS BRUTE: Really . . .?

MRS DRUDGE: You know the vicar?

MRS BRUTE: Not in the Biblical sense, no . . .

MRS DRUDGE: A charming man; very persuasive. God did well to get him. You know it was a choice between the Church and I.C.I.?

MRS BRUTE: Indeed?

MRS DRUDGE: I.C.I. pays better of course, but as he said, one has to take the broad view; the Church is the bigger organisation.

MRS BRUTE: Longer established of course.

MRS DRUDGE: Naturally. And expanding all the time.

MRS BRUTE: So is I.C.I.

MRS DRUDGE: But *they* only have the one world, you see. They don't have the connections in the hereafter.

MRS BRUTE: True. And in Russia.

MRS DRUDGE: True.

> [*Slight pause.*]

Well, well . . .

MRS BRUTE: Very true . . .

> [*Slight pause.* MRS DRUDGE *picks up her*
> *pocket diary.*]

MRS DRUDGE: I was looking through my pocket diary, Mrs Brute. I notice that the pheasant shooting is on us again.

MRS BRUTE: Indeed?

[*She goes to her bureau, finds her diary, and looks through it.*]

MRS DRUDGE: October 1st.

MRS BRUTE: You're right. It has quite passed me by.

MRS DRUDGE: It'll be with us till the first of February.

MRS BRUTE: A long season.

MRS DRUDGE: The same as usual.

MRS BRUTE: And what when it's over?

MRS DRUDGE: Well, now, the anniversary of the accession of Queen Elizabeth the Second, Queen of all England, is only five days later.

MRS BRUTE: That's a comfort. But wait. This means that it was necessary to renew one's gun licence, which expired on July 31st.

MRS DRUDGE: True. But you see, it probably *was* renewed for the opening of the grouse shooting, August 12th, and if not for that, then to fire a salute in honour of Queen Elizabeth the Queen Mother, August 4th, Her Royal Highness Princess Anne, August 15th, and *His* Royal Highness the Prince of Wales, November 14th.

MRS BRUTE: Christmas day?

MRS DRUDGE: Hardly. Fox-hunting, begins November 1st.

MRS BRUTE: With a gun?

MRS DRUDGE: Perhaps not.

[*Pause.*]

BOTH: I see the . . .

MRS DRUDGE: I beg your pardon.

MRS BRUTE: Do go on.

MRS DRUDGE: After you.

MRS BRUTE: I see the capital of Chile is Santiago.

MRS DRUDGE: Oh yes; and of Ecuador, Quito.

MRS BRUTE: Nicaragua, Managua, Liberia, Monrovia —

MRS DRUDGE: Guatemala, Guatemala, Venezuela, Caracas. One could go on indefinitely.

MRS BRUTE: It's the usual story. Look at the distances in miles between London and the principal towns. Aberdeen, 515, Birmingham, 110, *Liverpool,* 197 . . .

MRS DRUDGE: By road.

MRS BRUTE:	Pardon?
MRS DRUDGE:	By road, Mrs Brute. Not by rail. Let's be fair.
MRS BRUTE:	It's slightly less by rail, I agree. but it can be *more*.
MRS DRUDGE:	Or neither.
MRS BRUTE:	Neither?
MRS DRUDGE:	Stoke-on-Trent: 146 by road, 146 by rail.
MRS BRUTE:	A good point. But an isolated instance doesn't alter the main argument.
MRS DRUDGE:	True enough. On the other hand, consider the methods available for the removal of stains. Acetone for tobacco stains, sodium hypochlorite for mildew, ammonia and glycerine for blood . . .
MRS BRUTE:	And egg. Mrs Drudge.
MRS DRUDGE:	And egg. How to remove the ammonia and glycerine of course is not stated.
MRS BRUTE:	Say what you will, the simplest way to obliterate a stain is to cover it with marking ink.
MRS DRUDGE:	And what if the stain *is* marking ink?
MRS BRUTE:	One uses one's discretion. *Noblesse oblige*, Mrs Drudge.
MRS DRUDGE:	*Suaviter in modo, fortiter in re.* I'm sorry, have I said something out of place?
MRS BRUTE:	Nothing, nothing . . .
MRS DRUDGE:	You know, Mrs Brute, what I find so refreshing about these little tete-a-tetes, as we English say, is that we see eye to eye on so many things. Measures of capacity, geometrical formulae, coastal sea areas . . .
MRS BRUTE:	Seasonal work to be done in the garden . . .
MRS DRUDGE:	Commercial terms and phrases . . .
MRS BRUTE:	*Ad valorem.*
MRS DRUDGE:	*Pro rata.*
MRS BRUTE:	Collateral security.
MRS DRUDGE:	F.O.B. Ha, ha, those were the days . . .
MRS BRUTE:	That reminds me. Did I tell you about the Plantagenets?
	[*She leans over confidentially.*]
MRS DRUDGE:	No?
MRS BRUTE:	Well — it seems they'd been going since 1154.

They'd had Henrys and Richards, and Edwards and even a John ...

MRS DRUDGE: A what?

MRS BRUTE: A *John*. But then, in 1399, of all years — they couldn't even wait for the 1400s —

[*The door opens.* HILDA *comes in with the tea trolley.* MRS BRUTE *stops talking abruptly.*]

HILDA: Two points ...

[*As she speaks she wheels the trolley over to its place and begins to arrange things and check contents.*]

Point one: don't be taken in by the apparent concern for my innocence shown by the sudden silence on my entrance. The concern may be as real as you'll get within these four walls, but the innocence is another matter. Far be it from me, a simple below-stairs illiterate, to comment on the apparent paradoxicality of a system engendering simultaneously the most extreme delicacy in the conversation of the mistress in the presence of the maid, and the passing round of the said maid like a bag of sweets from one to another male member of the establishment, each one stripping off her hygenic wrappings and enjoying her after his own kind — the younger son as if chewing toffee, the elder son wolfing her down like a quarter of a pound of salted peanuts, smacking his lips and belching, the father savouring her with the jaded poise of a middle-aged Shakespearean actor eating liqueur chocolates with his port and cigars while being photographed as an advertisement for travel by Air France Epicurean — and finally the unmentionable friend, the archdevil himself, whose unspeakable diversity of vice defies metaphorical comparison with the eating of any known type of confectionery, but whose eventual discarding of the said maid can be likened to the behaviour of a small boy, who on finishing his bag of liquorice all sorts fills the bag with air, explodes it between his hands, tosses it into the lavatory pan and pulls the chain on it. Far be it from me as I say, to mention it. But as for the English succession, I know more about that than *they'll* ever know, Plantagenets and all. *And* the Commonwealth, 1649 — 1660. I know a bend sinister when I see one. Point two can wait.

MRS BRUTE: You may go.

HILDA: Yes, madam.

        [*She goes.*]

MRS DRUDGE: Twenty to seven.

MRS BRUTE: Ah.

        [*She tilts the face of the clock until it reads twenty to seven.*]

        Two things are troubling me, Mrs Drudge ...

MRS DRUDGE: Oh?

MRS BRUTE: Firstly — Tea?

MRS DRUDGE: Thank you.

MRS BRUTE: Firstly I was musing on England's greatness, on all those things which have made us what we are today, or were yesterday — Indian or China?

MRS DRUDGE: Indian, please.

MRS BRUTE: Radar, Brighton Pavilion, the independent nuclear deterrent, Martin Luther — Milk or lemon?

MRS DRUDGE: Milk please. Martin Luther was a German ...

MRS BRUTE: A Boche? But some of my best friends are Lutherans. Milk in first?

MRS DRUDGE: Milk in first, please.

MRS BRUTE: Alfred Lord Tennyson — How can we regain the splendour we have lost, Mrs Drudge? English or Jersey milk?

MRS DRUDGE: Jersey, please. You want to exhume Lord Tennyson?

MRS BRUTE: There must be something we can do. Sugar?

MRS DRUDGE: Yes, please. A revival of the ancient crafts, perhaps ...?

MRS BRUTE: Escutcheon-designing; reed-warbling and hatching — cane or beet sugar?

MRS DRUDGE: Venetian glass. Cane please.

MRS BRUTE: One lump?

MRS DRUDGE: Two lumps.

MRS BRUTE: Shall I stir it, or will you?

MRS DRUDGE: You stir it, Mrs Brute.

MRS BRUTE: Do you object to my stirring it with an apostle spoon?

MRS DRUDGE: Not at all.

MRS BRUTE: Clockwise or anticlockwise?

MRS DRUDGE: Clockwise, if you please. In the northern hemisphere.

MRS BRUTE: How many times?

MRS DRUDGE: I leave it to you.

MRS BRUTE: There.

[*They drink.*]

Is it to your liking?

MRS DRUDGE: A trifle strong.

MRS BRUTE: A little more milk?

MRS DRUDGE: Thank you.

MRS BRUTE: [*pausing*] But you like your milk in first.

MRS DRUDGE: It doesn't matter.

MRS BRUTE: Shall we start again with another cup?

MRS DRUDGE: No, really.

MRS BRUTE: Someone should stop the rot, one feels.

MRS DRUDGE: Rot?

MRS BRUTE: The withering of our fair land.

MRS DRUDGE: Well now, Mrs Brute, I don't think we should be defeatist. Let us not forget the strides we have taken.

MRS BRUTE: In which direction?

MRS DRUDGE: Direction is irrelevant. In any case, whatever the evidence, *we* know we're superior. What more does one want?

MRS BRUTE: But what about the dago, Mrs Drudge?

MRS DRUDGE: Who?

MRS BRUTE: All those people across the Channel — the frog, the hun and all the rest of them. Do *they* know?

MRS DRUDGE: We *have* told them.

MRS BRUTE: But do they listen? I sometimes honestly believe they think *they* are the superior ones. What's the use of having a great country if every *other* country thinks *it's* a great country? We should publish the facts Mrs Drudge.

MRS DRUDGE: Abroad?

MRS BRUTE: Of course. Tell them in plain English. In simple terms, of course. *Explain* to them we're greater than they are. With photographs, Mrs Drudge, to prove it. A radar station; the Tower of London, scene of so many historic assassinations . . .

MRS DRUDGE: The Royal Family with their dogs to show our love of animals.

MRS BRUTE: A foxhunt.

MRS DRUDGE: A staghunt.

MRS BRUTE: An otterhunt.

MRS DRUDGE: To show our love of sport.

MRS BRUTE: Cucumber or jam?

MRS DRUDGE: Thank you.

[HILDA *appears.*]

HILDA: [*winking broadly at the audience*] You rang, madam?

MRS BRUTE: Not in the least.

HILDA: Point two: footnote to the published text, being an elucidation of the plot. The character of Mrs Drudge, so finely and subtly drawn, is obviously of great significance. From certain veiled clues, various scholars have come to various conclusions. But can it be doubted that Mrs Drudge is in *fact* the *widow* of the notorious Maconochie, and that in 1932, when Mrs Brute, discovering, as she thought, that Maconochie was having an unnatural affair with her son — mistakenly of course since it was the maid they were all after — despatched her husband by hot-water bottle rather than that he should learn the truth, meaning to take her own life later, though as we know her own bottle failed to go off — Mrs Drudge, then Mrs Maconochie, having been herself in love with Mr Brute, and suspecting that Mrs Brute had done away with her husband when he discovered that she, Mrs Brute, was having an affair with *her* husband, Mr Maconochie, tried in despair to take her own life but by mistake took her husband's instead? This is the secret between them. Has Mrs Brute *really* lost her memory? What game is Mrs Drudge playing? Were the sons really daughters, and in that case why is the maid lying? What is the significance of the Eiffel Tower? Now read on.

MRS BRUTE: You may remove the trolley, Hilda.

HILDA: Yes, madam.

[*She goes out.*]

MRS DRUDGE: What was the other thing?

MRS BRUTE: What other thing?

MRS DRUDGE: You said two things were troubling you.

MRS BRUTE: What was the other thing?

MRS DRUDGE: England's greatness.

MRS BRUTE: Yes, yes. Did we finish it?

MRS DRUDGE: I think so.

MRS BRUTE: Good . . .

MRS DRUDGE: So what was the other thing?

MRS BRUTE: Shall we play cards?

MRS DRUDGE: Delightful.

[*They sit at cards.*]

MRS BRUTE: Cut for dealer.

[*She cuts.*]

MRS DRUDGE: I deal.

[*She deals five or six cards.*]

MRS BRUTE: Mhmm.

[*She throws down a card. The others follow alternately in quick succession.*]

Hard luck, Mrs Drudge.

MRS DRUDGE: Well, well . . . the night is young.

[*She takes off her hat and puts it on the floor beside her.* MRS BRUTE *shuffles.*]

MRS BRUTE: Cut please.

[MRS DRUDGE *cuts.* MRS BRUTE *deals.*]

MRS DRUDGE: *Oho.*

[*She throws down a card. The others follow alternately in quick succession.*]

Dear me, what a beginning.

MRS BRUTE: If you'd kept back the knave —

MRS DRUDGE: No post-mortems, Mrs Brute . . .

> [*She takes off a shoe, and shuffles.* MRS BRUTE *cuts.* MRS DRUDGE *deals.*]

MRS BRUTE: The other thing that was troubling me was this . . . talking of post-mortems . . . [*She looks at her cards.*] If I were to say to you, for the sake of argument . . . a certain name . . . My word, my luck is in tonight . . .

MRS DRUDGE: Which name?

MRS BRUTE: [*playing a card*] The ace of spades. The black one, master of us all.

> [*The remaining cards are played.*]

My game again.

MRS DRUDGE: I realise that.

> [*She takes off her other shoe.* MRS BRUTE *shuffles.*]

Which name, Mrs Brute?

MRS BRUTE: Hm?

MRS DRUDGE: Which *name*?

MRS BRUTE: Cut.

MRS DRUDGE: Cut?

MRS BRUTE: *Cut.*

> [MRS DRUDGE *cuts.* MRS BRUTE *deals.*]

If I were to say to you, for the sake of argument, the name . . . [*Looking at* MRS DRUDGE, *she says the names as she deals the cards*] . . . Hopkins . . . Grant . . . Pritchard . . . Smith . . . Maconochie . . . ?

> [MRS DRUDGE *looks at her cards. She throws one down.* MRS BRUTE *waits.*]

MRS DRUDGE: You to play, Mrs Brute . . .

MRS BRUTE: Hm . . .

> [*The cards are played.*]

MRS DRUDGE: My win.

> [MRS BRUTE *takes the kerchief from her neck. The game continues.*]

Everything evens itself out, of course. If one waits long enough.

MRS BRUTE: Mrs Drudge . . . Are you ever beset with a sense of
              . . . loss?

MRS DRUDGE: Of what?

MRS BRUTE: How does one know, when one's lost it? Let me
              put it to you this way, you're a woman of the
              world, Mrs Drudge, a widow, as I am. Very well.
              Here we sit, two women of the world, two widows,
              playing cards together on an October evening in
              the well-furnished drawing room of a detached
              house in the safety of Streatham, England. The
              government hasn't fallen, no invader roams the
              streets ready to break down the door and drag us
              off to unnamed horrors — the Queen is well —
              we've had tea . . . And as you say, if we play cards
              long enough it evens itself out, we lose equally . . .

MRS DRUDGE: My game.
                        [MRS BRUTE *kicks off one shoe.*]

MRS BRUTE: Mrs Drudge . . . do you remember your husband's
              face?

MRS DRUDGE: What about his face?

MRS BRUTE: Do you remember his *face*?

MRS DRUDGE: [*looking upwards*] My husband, Mrs Brute, was a
              man . . .

MRS BRUTE: I don't dispute that, Mrs Drudge, I merely asked
              . . .

MRS DRUDGE: My husband was — magnificent. Extraordinary.
              To me, anyway, what he was to others is not my
              concern. To me he was — You'd not understand.

MRS BRUTE: Why should I not understand?

MRS DRUDGE: Because he was unique. Unique, Mrs Brute . . .

MRS BRUTE: In what way was your husband unique?

MRS DRUDGE: I don't think I could explain to you . . .

MRS BRUTE: Did he have two heads?

MRS DRUDGE: No, he didn't have two heads. Two legs, two arms
              . . . *Your* husband, you see, if I may say so, was ob-
              viously not a . . .

MRS BRUTE: Not a what?

MRS DRUDGE: Not a man of — passionate nature.

MRS BRUTE: You mean he was not violent?

MRS DRUDGE: I mean he was not passionate in his nature and in
              — himself . . .
MRS BRUTE: In *himself?* Why do you come to that conclusion?
MRS DRUDGE: I look at you, Mrs Brute, and I come to that con-
              clusion.
MRS BRUTE: That my husband was not passionate in himself?
              While yours was?
MRS DRUDGE: Do you doubt it?
MRS BRUTE: Looking at you, Mrs Drudge . . .
MRS DRUDGE: Mrs Brute . . . You have no *conception* — how
              passionate my husband was in himself . . . *My
              win.* Your other shoe, Mrs Brute . . .
              [MRS BRUTE *takes off her other shoe.*]
MRS BRUTE: It doesn't show — Mrs Drudge.
MRS DRUDGE: The effect is perhaps too profound for you to
              notice.
              [*Shuffling and dealing,* MRS BRUTE
              laughs.]
              Why do you laugh?
MRS BRUTE: That you can say my husband was not passionate
              in himself. My dear Mrs Drudge . . .
MRS DRUDGE: You may have thought so . . .
MRS BRUTE: *I* may have *thought* so!
              [*She rings the bell.* HILDA *appears.*]
HILDA: You . . . ?
MRS BRUTE: Hilda, what kind of man was my husband?
              [HILDA *opens her mouth, not sure what to
              say.*]
              Was he a passionate man, would you say?
HILDA: [*flatly*] Yes, madam.
MRS BRUTE: In himself?
HILDA: Yes, madam.
MRS BRUTE: You may go.
              [HILDA *goes. They play.*]
              My win. Your jacket, Mrs Drudge.
              [MRS DRUDGE *takes off her jacket.*]
              If you could have seen what used to go on — in
              this very room . . .
MRS DRUDGE: You think I'd have been surprised?

MRS BRUTE:	You'd have been astounded, Mrs Drudge ... Struck dumb.
MRS DRUDGE:	You flatter yourself.
MRS BRUTE:	I flatter my *husband* — No, he was above flattery. Superb, superb ...
MRS DRUDGE:	My husband was ...
MRS BRUTE:	*Your husband!* Your miserable lap-dog! Look at you! Untouched! Unmarked! Like a blank sheet of paper. No, I'll tell you what you're like; you're like a single bed in a dusty attic.
MRS DRUDGE:	Mrs Brute ...
MRS BRUTE:	A two-foot bed in an unused attic, long-covered with a thin film of dust. It's quite obvious you've never had a proper experience in your life.
MRS DRUDGE:	What! Untouched! Do you see that? Do you know what that is? A broken collar-bone! It didn't set properly; it was broken in two places. Do you think I broke it playing football?
MRS BRUTE:	The collar-bone is the easiest bone to break ...
MRS DRUDGE:	I see. And what do you have? A broken thigh? Very well, let's see it. Let's see your broken thigh!
MRS BRUTE:	This is what I have! Do you see this couch? Examine it closely. Look — the springs are broken. Every one of them. Broken, shattered ... destroyed. This couch was made by the most reliable firm in England. I keep it for a keepsake. I don't need broken collar-bones. And I didn't play football on this couch either.
	[*She rings the bell.* HILDA *appears.*]
	Hilda, what's wrong with this couch?
HILDA:	It's broken, madam.
MRS BRUTE:	How did it get broken?
HILDA:	I don't know, madam.
MRS BRUTE:	Did anyone play football on it?
HILDA:	No, madam.
MRS BRUTE:	Jump on it from the top of a wardrobe? Drop a piano on it?
HILDA:	Not to my knowledge, madam.
MRS BRUTE:	You may go.

[HILDA *goes. Pause.* MRS DRUDGE *shrugs.*]

MRS DRUDGE: He was presumably an angular man. *My* husband would not have used the couch. He'd have found it too small. He liked to spread himself, he needed *room.*

MRS BRUTE: For what, to sleep?

MRS DRUDGE: Not to sleep, Mrs Brute, to make *love!* To make love — again, and again, and again . . .

MRS BRUTE: How many times?

MRS DRUDGE: You can keep that thing as a keepsake. Our bed it was impossible to keep. It was smashed to smithereens.

MRS BRUTE: How many . . . ?

MRS DRUDGE: Four.

MRS BRUTE: *Four!*

MRS DRUDGE: Six.

MRS BRUTE: Eight?

MRS DRUDGE: Yes, eight!

MRS BRUTE: Twelve?

MRS DRUDGE: The figure's ludicrous! Paltry!

[MRS BRUTE *rings.* HILDA *appears.*]

MRS BRUTE: Hilda, how many times? Fourteen?

HILDA: Yes, madam.

MRS BRUTE: Twenty-two?

HILDA: Yes, madam. As many as you like.

MRS BRUTE: Was there any *end* to it?

HILDA: No, madam, no end to it. May I go, madam?

[MRS BRUTE *waves her out. Pause.*]

MRS DRUDGE: My husband . . . !

[*She subsides. They go back to the card-table.*]

Whose deal?

MRS BRUTE: Can you?

MRS DRUDGE: What?

MRS BRUTE: Remember his face?

MRS DRUDGE: Whose?

MRS BRUTE: Your husband's.

[*Pause.* MRS DRUDGE *shakes her head.*]

MRS DRUDGE: No . . .

MRS BRUTE: So it was possibly not your husband at all.
MRS DRUDGE: Possibly.
MRS BRUTE: Possibly — no-one.
MRS DRUDGE: Possibly. And you.
[*Pause.*]
What was his name again?
MRS BRUTE: Hilary — [*She thinks.*] — Macdonald ...
[*Pause.*]
MRS DRUDGE: It's very difficult — when one has so many memories — to remember them all.

THE END

PLAY FOR YESTERDAY

or

THE LITTLE HUT OF ENMITY

Characters

ELSPETH
JUSTIN
ILSE
MAISIE
MIKE
OLD KURT
YOUNG KURT

Play for Yesterday was written for the Richmond Fringe and first performed by them at the Orange Tree Theatre, Richmond, on 23 August, 1974. The cast was as follows:

ELSPETH	Diana Payan
JUSTIN	Richard Steele
MIKE	Derek Seaton
MAISIE	Janet Bartley
ILSE	Jonina Scott
OLD KURT	Jestyn Phillips

It was directed by Sam Walters.

A mountain hut.

Outside a blizzard is raging. Two figures approach with great difficulty, bending double against the wind. One is JUSTIN, *an English stockbroker. The other is his wife,* ELSPETH, *who is suffering from snow blindness and a frost-bitten foot.*

ELSPETH: It's no good, Justin. I can't go on. I must rest.

JUSTIN: We must keep going, Elspeth. It can't be far now.

ELSPETH: I just want to lie down in the snow.

JUSTIN: No. If we rest now we're done for.

ELSPETH: I'm so tired. Leave me here, Justin, you go on.

JUSTIN: Wait!

ELSPETH: What is it!

JUSTIN: There. Ahead. Look. That shape. Through the snow. It looks like ... It is. It's the hut. We've made it!

ELSPETH: Where?

JUSTIN: There, there. Don't you see?

ELSPETH: I can't see — anything. Just a swirling whiteness. Oh my God! My eyes are gone.

JUSTIN: Hold on to me. Just a few minutes now. We've got to make it, we've got to.

[*After enormous struggles they reach the hut, open the door and fall inside, slamming the door after them. The wind cuts to a low sound. Panting, the two collapse on the floor.*]

Are you all right, Elspeth ... ? I said are you all right?

ELSPETH: What do you care? What does anyone care?

JUSTIN: What do you mean by that?

ELSPETH: What do you think I mean?

JUSTIN: How the devil do I know what you mean!

ELSPETH: Oh God.

JUSTIN: Well, at least we're in shelter. We should be safe ... for a while. We have time to rest; to consider the situation.

ELSPETH: Time to think.
[*She gives a hollow laugh.*]

JUSTIN: For God's sake hang onto yourself. Don't go to pieces now.

ELSPETH: Why? Would it embarrass you?

JUSTIN: Don't be a fool.

ELSPETH: You've always been embarrassed by me, haven't you, Justin? Afraid I'll show you up in front of your stockbroker friends. Well, we're alone here, you don't have to worry. Alone, just we two, like in the old days, in Daddy's summerhouse, remember?
[*She laughs mockingly.*]

JUSTIN: God, you know how to hurt, don't you? You know how to twist the knife.

ELSPETH: One thing I don't understand.

JUSTIN: What's that?

ELSPETH: Why didn't you leave me out there? In the snow? You'd be rid of me then, once and for all.

JUSTIN: You'd like that, wouldn't you? You'd like me to carry that on my conscience with all the rest; your murder.

ELSPETH: I see; it was your conscience you were thinking of, not me. I quite understand.

JUSTIN: Elspeth, I don't think a mountain hut in the middle of a blizzard is the best place to discuss our marital problems. And let me say this: I don't give a damn what you think of me any more, not now, not after all that's happened. Not after fifteen years of marriage, to each other; with all that implies . . .

ELSPETH: What do you mean by that?

JUSTIN: You know damn well what I mean.

ELSPETH: You despise me, don't you, Justin? You always have, ever since that first moment, when you took that speck out of my eye, remember? Pretending you were a doctor . . .

JUSTIN: Elspeth, can't you ever forget the past?

ELSPETH: Oh, you'd like that, wouldn't you?

JUSTIN: What do you mean by that?

ELSPETH: Oh, what's the use ... ?

JUSTIN: We can't go on like this. We're destroying one another. All I ask is that you give some thought to the other members of the party when they get here ...

ELSPETH: Don't you mean if? They may all be lying dead in the snow now: old Kurt, young Kurt, Maisie, Mike, Ilse ... There'll be just us two. My God, that would be ironical. I need another drink.

JUSTIN: Don't you think you've had enough?

ELSPETH: No I don't! I need another drink! Please ...

JUSTIN: Oh, what's the difference? Here ...

> [*He takes out his hip flask. She grabs it and drinks greedily.*]

Steady.

> [*She coughs.*]

ELSPETH: That's better. God, I'm tired.

JUSTIN: How's the foot?

ELSPETH: What do you care?

JUSTIN: See if you can move it.

ELSPETH: I can't. I can't move it! Justin, I can't feel my foot!

JUSTIN: Steady, steady. Here, let me look ...

ELSPETH: Oh God!

JUSTIN: Yes, it looks ugly. I shall have to cut the boot off. This may hurt a little.

> [*He does so. She cries out.*]

There. That'll ease the pain till we can get you to a doctor.

ELSPETH: You're very good to me, Justin.

JUSTIN: You don't believe that.

ELSPETH: Oh, but you are. I don't know why. You'll get Daddy's money in any case.

JUSTIN: My God, you're a bitch.

> [*He goes to the window and looks out.*]

ELSPETH: I'm sorry. That was a vile thing to say. Sometimes I feel as if I've been taken over, as if I'm — somebody else. I can't stand any more, Justin, I think I'm going mad ...

JUSTIN: Steady, old girl.

ELSPETH: No sign of the others?

JUSTIN: No. It's all the fault of that bloody guide!

ELSPETH: Old Kurt?

JUSTIN: Young Kurt. To run off like that. Breaking down, losing control, swearing at his fiancee, it makes one ashamed of being human.

ELSPETH: Poor boy. Such a young, young, young, young man ...

JUSTIN: Yes, you would say that.

ELSPETH: Why would I say that? What do you mean?

JUSTIN: Do I have to spell it out?

ELSPETH: You're vile, Justin. You're sick, ill, unbalanced. Fifteen years I've had of your insane jealousies.

JUSTIN: Insane, are they?

ELSPETH: The outpourings of your sick mind, the outward manifestations of your basic sense of insecurity.

JUSTIN: You're crazy.

ELSPETH: And all because you've never been able to —

JUSTIN: Stop it, for God's sake! Don't say something we'll both regret.

ELSPETH: No, I won't say it. We haven't mentioned it for fifteen years. It's too late now ...

JUSTIN: But don't you find it strange, Elspeth, that only with you, in private, am I the creature of insane fantasies you make me out to be? Our friends —

ELSPETH: Friends! What friends?
[*She laughs.*]

JUSTIN: All right, we have no friends. Do you want me to spell out why?

ELSPETH: I don't give a damn.

JUSTIN: The reason we've lost all our friends is, firstly, the way you make up to every man you meet, married or single —

ELSPETH: You're mad. Mad!

JUSTIN: And secondly, the drink.

ELSPETH: Do you remember the night I started drinking, Justin, that night in San Remo? Look at me! Do you remember what it was you did? And what you didn't do ... ? I hate you, Justin. Do you know that?

JUSTIN: I have a vague inkling.

ELSPETH: I hate you with a deep and abiding hatred. I don't think anyone has ever hated anyone the way I hate you. Sometimes I think it's the only real thing left, this hate, the only thing keeping me sane.

JUSTIN: Sane ... ?

[*He laughs.*]

ELSPETH: I don't want to talk any more, I don't want to feel any more. I'm empty, drained.

JUSTIN: Yet it was you insisted that we come on this holiday.

ELSPETH: Holiday ...

[*She laughs.*]

JUSTIN: I told you it wouldn't work. But once you're obsessed with an idea —

ELSPETH: All right, I was wrong. Wrong to try again just one last time. Wrong not to give up and end it all. Wrong to think possibly if I really and truly tried I might come to some faint glimmering of an understanding of what it is that makes it such hell for us to live together. Wrong to — oh God! Suddenly nothing seems to matter any more ... What are these mountains doing to us?

JUSTIN: Mountains?

ELSPETH: It's almost as if there's a —

JUSTIN: What?

ELSPETH: Don't laugh. As if they're ... judging us.

JUSTIN: You feel that too?

[*A distant cry.*]

Listen!

ELSPETH: What?

JUSTIN: I thought I heard ... Listen!

[*Pause. Silence except for the muffled blizzard.*]

No, nothing.

ELSPETH: Justin ... Do you think there's still a chance for us?

JUSTIN:	Do you mean together? Or to survive?
ELSPETH:	I don't know. I don't know anything any more. It's these mountains. They make me feel suddenly terribly small. It's ironical really.
JUSTIN:	What is?
	[Distant voices are heard calling.]
ELSPETH:	Listen.
JUSTIN:	What is it?
ELSPETH:	I thought I heard someone calling my name.
JUSTIN:	Imagination. One gets like that in the mountains.
ELSPETH:	No. There it is again.
	[Closer voices are heard calling.]
JUSTIN:	It's old Kurt! Good old Kurt!
	[A moment later the door is flung open.]
	Maisie! Ilse! You made it!
ILSE:	Vot did you expect?
ELSPETH:	Mike. Old Kurt. Thank God, thank God ...
	[She breaks down.]
MIKE:	This sure is some storm. I never knew anything like this back in the States.
JUSTIN:	You surprise me.
MIKE:	We got mountains, you know.
JUSTIN:	Bigger than these, I daresay.
ELSPETH:	Stop it, you two, stop it!
MIKE:	God-damned Limey ...
	[He takes out a mouth organ and begins to play.]
MAISIE:	God, that wind. It's almost as if it knows we're in here. It's out there, waiting, waiting for us, like a ...
MIKE:	Take it easy, Maisie.
ILSE:	Ze mountains are testing us.
JUSTIN:	What's that, Ilse?
ILSE:	Zey try our strength. Zey do not like veak people.
JUSTIN:	Damn it, Ilse, are you referring to ...?
ILSE:	You vill see. It vill go on for days, perhaps veeks, till the veak are vinkled out.
ELSPETH:	Oh God ...
	[OLD KURT is mumbling to himself and

groaning, in Swiss German.]

JUSTIN: Get up, old Kurt. Why are you grovelling there on the floor?

MIKE: Leave him alone.

JUSTIN: Are you addressing me?

MIKE: I said leave the old man alone.

JUSTIN: When I want your advice I'll ask for it.

MIKE: You arrogant limey bastard —

JUSTIN: Take your hands off me!
[*They fight.*]

ELSPETH: Stop it! For the love of God stop it! We're beginning to behave like animals!

MIKE: She's right. Look, Justin, I know you don't like me. For the matter of that, I don't like you either. I don't like you one little bit. Not one little bit I don't.

JUSTIN: I get the message.

MIKE: But if we're to be cooped up in this hut for any length of time I suggest we do the best we can to try and not get in each other's hair more than we humanly have to.

JUSTIN: That makes sense.

MIKE: I'm glad you think so.

JUSTIN: Look, Mr —

MIKE: Nobody calls me Mr. The name's Mike.

JUSTIN: Look, I'm willing to call a truce for the sake of the ladies.

MAISIE: Say, does that include me?

JUSTIN: I'll try not to get in your hair, as you put it, if you'll try not to get into mine.

MIKE: It's a bargain. But I still say leave old Kurt alone.

ELSPETH: What's the matter with him? Is he hurt?

ILSE: He is too old, zat is vot is ze matter viz him. He should not be here. Ze mountains are for ze young and ze strong, not ze old and ze veak who hold us back vhen ve vant to go forward.

MIKE: So what would you do? Liquidate everyone over forty, I suppose.

JUSTIN: Yes, just what the hell do you mean, Ilse?

ILSE: You British and Americans vould not understand.

MIKE: Now see here —!

JUSTIN: Steady, Mike.

MIKE: Say, you called me Mike.

JUSTIN: A slip of the tongue.

MIKE: Sure . . .

JUSTIN: So what *is* the matter with old Kurt?

MIKE: Young Kurt, of course.

MAISIE: You mean —?

MIKE: Yeah. You got it.

JUSTIN: It's a bad business.

ELSPETH: I don't understand. Is . . .?

MIKE: You ask if he's hurt. Sure he's hurt, deep down inside. He's suffering from shame, you see. Shame for his son.

ELSPETH: But how . . .?

MIKE: Don't you see? He comes on the trip against all advice, an eighty-year-old man with a withered arm . . .

JUSTIN: You mean you think . . .?

MIKE: Sure. He came out here to die. That's the way I see it.

MAISIE: Elephants do that.

MIKE: Shut up, Maisie. It's not good to grow old in the mountains. Not if you were once young, as he was. Oh yes, he was young once. Now there's nothing left. His wife is gone, disappeared in the mountains. All he has left is the memory of his youth, his virility, which he projects onto that son of his.

ELSPETH: Young Kurt.

MIKE: Sure, young Kurt. He can only be young again through his son, by leaving a son just like him to carry on when he leaves off.

JUSTIN: But his son —

MIKE: Sure. His son's a cissy.

ELSPETH: Don't use that word.

JUSTIN: Face the facts, Elspeth, for God's sake, for once in your life. He ran away. He's a coward. A mountain guide who's terrified of heights, it's ironical.

ELSPETH: You're vile, Justin.

MIKE: Don't get me wrong. I'm not blaming him for being what he is. We're all what we are, that's the way I see it; deep down inside —

JUSTIN: I disagree. We're free individuals, we have the ability to rise above ourselves.

ELSPETH: Justin believes in the supremacy of the will, Mike. Perhaps he should have married Ilse rather than me, they'd have got on very well together. Perhaps I should have married you, Mike. [*She laughs hollowly.*]

JUSTIN: Can we keep our domestic affairs out of this just for once?

MIKE: Look, the way I see it is this: somewhere deep down inside we're all afraid of something. Every one of us. Me, you, your wife Elspeth, young Kurt, old Kurt, Maisie, even that tall blonde Aryan there, the beautiful Ilse . . .

ILSE: Ach! [*She swears in Swiss German.*]

MIKE: Oh, we put on a front, puff out our chests, don't we, Ilse? But deep down inside we're afraid.

JUSTIN: Of what?

MIKE: That one day it'll come out into the open.

ELSPETH: You mean . . .?

MIKE: What we're afraid of, right.

ELSPETH: What are you afraid of, Mike?

MIKE: Ah, that would be telling. Maybe cooped up here together, maybe for days, maybe for ever, maybe we'll all learn each other's secrets. And it won't be pretty.

ILSE: You talk nonsense. It is simple. Ze strong get to ze top. Ze veak go to ze vall. Zat is ze vay it is and zat is ze vay it should be.

MIKE: Sure, that's what Hitler thought, didn't he?

JUSTIN: Steady, Mike.

ELSPETH: I'm beginning to understand. You mean that old Kurt came on this trip to give his strength to young Kurt, hoping against hope he could conquer his fear of heights, so that he could die in peace knowing he could take over?

MIKE: That's the way I see it. Look at it this way: deep down inside us —

MAISIE: But he made him like that.

ELSPETH: Who made who like what?

MAISIE: Old Kurt. Don't you see, he's driven young Kurt into trying to be what he is, but he's not and never was and never can be. He's destroyed him as surely as if he actually killed him.

JUSTIN: I think perhaps she's onto something there.

MIKE: Maybe you're not quite so dumb as you look.

JUSTIN: And of course he knows!

ELSPETH: Who knows?

JUSTIN: Old Kurt!

ELSPETH: Of course. And blames himself?

JUSTIN: And that's why —!

ELSPETH: My God, we've been so blind, so blind!

MIKE: Not only that . . .

JUSTIN: Something else?

MIKE: He thinks he's dead.

JUSTIN: Old Kurt?

MIKE: Young Kurt.

ELSPETH: You mean old Kurt thinks young Kurt is dead?

MIKE: There was a cry. At least he says he thought he heard a cry. You can never be sure in the mountains. He'd heard a cry like that only once before in his life: the day his wife disappeared down a crack in the glacier.

ELSPETH: It's horrible, horrible!

MAISIE: But that means . . .!

JUSTIN: Yes. It's ironical, isn't it.

[OLD KURT *grunts and groans, muttering to himself, as he hauls himself painfully to his feet.*]

ELSPETH: He's trying to get up.

JUSTIN: Sit down, old man; you've done all you could.

[OLD KURT *speaks in Swiss German.*]

MIKE: What's he saying?

ILSE: He says he apologises for ze inconvenience. He says that now his son is gone he is in charge. He says ve are to do exactly as he says. He says ve are not to vorry, he vill see us through.

JUSTIN: He's got guts, I'll say that for him.

[ILSE *speaks to* OLD KURT *in Swiss German.*]

MIKE: What's she saying?

JUSTIN: Who knows? It's this particular dialect of Swiss German. It's only spoken in these mountains. They were cut off, you know, for hundreds of years, from all contact with the outside world when a mountain fell across their valley. They're a strange, proud people. Simple, ignorant, treacherous, intolerant, avaricious and yet — there's something, some quality . . .

MIKE: I know what you mean. There's an old legend about this mountain, you know.

JUSTIN: The legless skier . . .

MIKE: You've heard it too.

MAISIE: What is it? Tell us.

MIKE: Well, the story goes —

JUSTIN: Mike, do you think this is the right moment?

ELSPETH: We're not children, Justin.

JUSTIN: As you wish.

MIKE: Well, the story goes —

[ILSE *and* OLD KURT *are arguing, their voices raised.* OLD KURT *slaps her face. She swears and spits.*]

JUSTIN: Good God, he struck her!

MIKE: Say, what's going on?

ELSPETH: What were you saying to him?

ILSE: Ze truth. I told him he is old, finished. I said his place is in ze village, stirring his pot. I said I take control now. I said his family is rotten, veak and decadent, zey are not fit for ze mountains. I said it is good zat his son fell down ze crack in ze glacier.

MIKE: My God!

ELSPETH: And he hit you?

ILSE: Ja. He has still some of ze man in him.
[*She looks at* OLD KURT *with a mixture of admiration and contempt.*]

JUSTIN: Even so, to strike a woman ...

ELSPETH: But Ilse, you were young Kurt's *fiancee* ...

ILSE: You are wrong. I vas not his fiancee, I vas his ... *vife.*

MIKE: Well I'll be ...

JUSTIN: Good grief!

MAISIE: So that's why ...

ELSPETH: It makes one ashamed to be a woman ...

ILSE: Ashamed? Vot do you know? You understand nossing! Nossing! How can you know vot it is to be a voman in ze mountains! You — you —!

JUSTIN: Leave my wife alone! Can't you see she's suffering from snow-blindness and a frostbitten foot?

ELSPETH: Thank you Justin, but I can take care of myself.

MAISIE: I've had enough of this! My God, you make me sick, you people.

MIKE: Maisie —

MAISIE: Shut up, Mike. You educated people, you decadent middle-class bourgeoisie, sitting on your fat backsides. Do you have any idea what people are really like?

JUSTIN: My God, a communist ...

MAISIE: Yes, a communist! And proud of it! Wouldn't you be if your mother had had to struggle and scrape to bring up eleven kids in an attic? With my father drunk in the corner and nothing to eat but what we could scrape off the floor? Is it any wonder I grew up to be what I am?

ELSPETH: And we all know what that is.

MAISIE: Yes, I'm a whore! I'm not afraid to say it, I'll shout it from the mountain top. I am a whore! And proud of it! Proud that I managed to drag myself out of the gutter, from under the heel of the capitalist oppressor and make something of myself, yes, proud, do you hear?!
[*She breaks down.*]

ELSPETH: Maisie, I'm sorry, I didn't realise . . .

MAISIE: I don't want your pity! You think you're so superior, Mrs Montgomery-Clift-Parkinson or whatever your name is, but you don't fool me. I can read you like a book!

MIKE: You can't read, Maisie . . .

MAISIE: You keep out of this. Yes, I know your trouble: jealousy! And I'll tell you why you're jealous: because you're frigid. A frigid middle-class bitch. You put on airs in your smart new ski-pants, but I'll bet you've never had a real man in your life!

ELSPETH: You cow!

JUSTIN: Ignore her, Elspeth . . .

MAISIE: As for you, don't think I haven't noticed you watching me, felt your eyes on me, undressing me.

JUSTIN: Damn you! You're going too far!

MAISIE: And did you tell your precious Elspeth what happened that time the ski-lift broke down?

JUSTIN: That's a damned lie!

MAISIE: Ask him! Go on, ask him what happened above the nursery slopes!

MIKE: Maisie, cut it out!

MAISIE: Not that he's the only one. They've all come to me, while you were playing the lady in your Paris gowns: Mike, Justin, young Kurt, old Kurt —

JUSTIN: Take no notice, Elspeth, she's insane.

ELSPETH: Yes, you'd say that.

JUSTIN: What do you mean by that?

ELSPETH: Do I have to spell it out? As for you, Maisie, you think your life was hard, but have you ever lost a —

JUSTIN: Elspeth! For God's sake!

ELSPETH: Don't worry. I won't say it. I lost control for a moment. I'm all right now.

JUSTIN: Steady, old girl.

MAISIE: Look, I'm sorry . . . I didn't mean any of that.

ELSPETH: I'm sorry too. We both said too much. Let's leave it at that. God, I'm so tired . . .

MAISIE: It's as if we're being taken over; as if we're being — used by somebody for something . . .

MIKE: As if the legend were repeating itself ... These God-damned mountains ...

[*He starts to play his mouth organ.*]

JUSTIN: Elspeth ... That night in the ski-lift —

ELSPETH: [*gently*] It's all right, Justin; it's all right ...

JUSTIN: I'd like to explain.

ELSPETH: There's no need. I knew, you see.

JUSTIN: Nothing happened, Elspeth.

ELSPETH: I know.

[*She looks at him in a new way.*]

JUSTIN: What cool hands you have ...

ELSPETH: Justin ... When old Kurt hit Ilse — did you notice something odd?

JUSTIN: Odd?

ELSPETH: I'd swear he hit her with his right arm; his withered arm ...

JUSTIN: I know.

ELSPETH: You saw?

JUSTIN: Yes.

ELSPETH: What does it mean?

JUSTIN: I don't know — yet ... Elspeth, if we ever get out of here, there's something I think you ought to know. I wanted to tell you for fifteen years but somehow never got around to it.

ELSPETH: Go on.

JUSTIN: It's hard to put it into words. Language is such an inadequate way of saying things.

ELSPETH: Try. Perhaps that's been our trouble: we've never quite put into words all the things we should have said to each other.

JUSTIN: You may be right. Sometimes I wonder if ...

ELSPETH: What?

JUSTIN: No, nothing.

ELSPETH: What were you going to tell me?

JUSTIN: It's this — no, don't look at me, I can tell it better if you don't — look at me.

ELSPETH: Poor Justin, you're such a child ...

JUSTIN: When I was a young lad, Elspeth, I was alone in the house one day ... I needed a piece of string, I forget what for. I went into the butler's pantry.

Phelps the butler was standing at the table. He was sharpening a carving knife and — I've never told this to a living soul — he was — naked . . .

[OLD KURT *gives a gutteral exclamation.*]

MIKE: What's the matter with Old Kurt?

[ILSE *speaks to* OLD KURT.]

OLD KURT: [*in Swiss German*] Ssch!

MAISIE: What is it? What has he heard?

ILSE: Ssch!

[*There is a long pause as they all listen for they know not what.*]

ELSPETH: Oh, Justin, I'm afraid.

JUSTIN: We're all afraid, I think.

ELSPETH: Even you?

[OLD KURT *says something.*]

ILSE: Ach! So! Mein Gott!

MAISIE: Oh, God, I'm frightened. I don't want to die, Mike, not yet.

MIKE: Take it easy, Maisie.

JUSTIN: For God's sake what is he saying, Ilse?

ILSE: He says ze snow is moving. At ze top of ze mountain, above ze glacier, by ze north face, by ze peaks of ze three old men . . .

JUSTIN: He can hear that?

ILSE: He has mountain ears. He hears vot ozzers do not. Ve must believe him. Zeze mountains are his children and his parents. It is necessary to keep absolutely still. Ze slightest vibration . . .

MIKE: So, Ilse, the old man's not so useless after all.

ILSE: Ach so . . .

ELSPETH: Justin, I'm afraid.

JUSTIN: Hold on to me, darling. Hold very tightly to me.

ILSE: Don't move!

[*A long pause.*]

MIKE: We'll crack up if we go on like this. Listen, I've got an idea.

MAISIE: I know your ideas.

MIKE: Shut up, Maisie. Listen, why don't we each in turn tell the others why we're here?

MAISIE: You're joking.

MIKE: Scared to, Maisie?

MAISIE: Me? [*She laughs.*]

JUSTIN: You mean — the truth game.

MIKE: You could call it that. Or you could call it a kind of verbal — Russian roulette.

JUSTIN: I really don't think —

ELSPETH: Justin, don't you see? This could be the way out!

JUSTIN: What do you mean?

ELSPETH: Don't you understand? God, you're so blind, so blind . . .

JUSTIN: Very well. I'm game.

MIKE: Good for you. Who'll start?

JUSTIN: Wait. We haven't yet heard whether the brave Ilse is willing to enter the game.

ILSE: Ich?

ELSPETH: Yes, Ilse, you?

ILSE: Ach . . .

MAISIE: Unless you're afraid to.

ILSE: Ich? Afraid? [*She laughs.*]

MIKE: Right, we're all agreed then.

MAISIE: What about the old man?

ILSE: He must stay listening for ze snow.

MAISIE: Right, I'll begin. Are you all sitting comfortably? Pin your ears back, then, and get a load of this: Picture to yourself a New Orleans brothel —

JUSTIN: Wait!

MIKE: What?

JUSTIN: My God, what fools we are! What blind, unthinking, unfeeling, self-centred fools!

ELSPETH: What is it?

MAISIE: Say, do you want to hear my story or not?

MIKE: Shut up, Maisie. What's biting you, Justin?

JUSTIN: Young Kurt! Young Kurt!

MIKE: What about him? He's dead.

JUSTIN: How do you know?

MIKE: What are you getting at?

JUSTIN: Who saw him die?

MIKE: Listen, he ran off into the blizzard, didn't he? There isn't a guy alive could live out there.

ILSE: He is dead. You know nossing of ze mountains.

Did ve not hear a cry as he fell down ze crack in ze glacier?

JUSTIN: Who heard it? Did you, Mike?

MIKE: Well, no . . .

JUSTIN: Elspeth?

ELSPETH: No.

JUSTIN: Maisie?

MAISIE: Not me.

ILSE: He heard it. Old Kurt.

JUSTIN: We have only your word for that. Strange, isn't it, if you're the only person to hear it?

ILSE: Is not strange. I too have mountain ears. I hear vot ozzers do not.

MIKE: Too right you do.

ELSPETH: Justin, you don't mean — ?

JUSTIN: Just answer me this, Ilse — as you are pleased to call yourself — What was your father doing in March 1943?

ILSE: Ach, Gott. How do you know — ?

JUSTIN: Never mind how I know, I know, that's all, I just happen to know. My God, your name's no more Ilse Baumeister than mine is.

MIKE: What is all this?

JUSTIN: I'll tell you later, Mike. She knows what I'm talking about.

ILSE: I know nossing. You are mad.

JUSTIN: Maybe I am. But by God, I'd like to have a good talk with young Kurt; or with old Kurt for that matter. You'd hate that, wouldn't you?

MIKE: I thought you were a funny kind of a stockbroker, Justin . . .

JUSTIN: Mike: have you ever heard of The Razor?

MIKE: The Razor? The German hero of the resistance movement? The man who — ?

JUSTIN: Not German, Mike. Swiss! Oh, it's all becoming clear.

MIKE: You mean the Neo-Nazis are . . .?

JUSTIN: Exactly. And because young Kurt speaks English, and could talk . . .

ELSPETH: What are you getting at, Justin?

JUSTIN: I think everyone in this room is quite aware what I'm getting at. Especially — that woman there!

ILSE: You are mad. Mad.

JUSTIN: But all this is beside the point. We are wasting valuable time. Whatever he is or was or may be, there is a man somewhere out there who may be still alive; or if he's dead, is dead because of us, because we were too — cowardly to go after him and bring him back.

ELSPETH: Justin, you don't mean to — !

JUSTIN: Yes. I'm going out there to bring him back. Dead or alive.

ILSE: You cannot. It is death out there. You know nossing of ze mountains.

MIKE: Listen, if anyone's going out there it'll be me. You're married, I've got no-one. There's not a soul alive in this whole god-damned rotten world would give a damn if I were never seen again. I'll go.

MAISIE: No! Not you! No!

[*She runs to him.*]

MIKE: Maisie . . .?

MAISIE: Let me go. I've got nothing to live for. Let me do something useful for once in my rotten, rotten life.

[*She breaks down.*]

MIKE: Maisie . . . I didn't realise . . .

JUSTIN: No, I shall go. It's the logical choice. Don't you see, we owe it to old Kurt.

ELSPETH: Justin — oh, Justin . . .

JUSTIN: You're quite right about me, you know. You always have been. Everything you've ever said about me has been the plain, unvarnished truth. My God, only now do I begin to see it. No, I think I always knew. Now I can admit it. I'm rotten, Elspeth, I always have been. My God, what it must have been like living with me. No, don't say anything, let me finish. Elspeth — if I don't come back —

ELSPETH: No!

JUSTIN: Steady, old girl. Let's face the truth for the first time in our lives. If I don't come back, all I ask is this, not that I have any right to ask anything of you. Remember me as I am now; not that hollow sham you lived with all those years, but a man doing, for the first time in his life, the decent thing. Remember me as I am when I go through that door.

[*He steps to the door.*]

I may be some time.

[*He opens the door. The blizzard howls in. He makes a superhuman effort, trying to force himself into the wind.*]

The wind, it's too ... I can't ...

[*With a cry he collapses back, sobbing with frustration. The door slams shut.*]

I can't deal with the wind! Oh, God, I'm too weak! Too weak!

ELSPETH: Oh, Justin, I do love you: do, do, love you ...

JUSTIN: I'm weak, weak ...

ELSPETH: No, Justin, you're strong, strong. Strong enough to know that you are weak. That is the greatest strength of all.

JUSTIN: Look after me, Elspeth. Take care of me. Don't leave me.

ELSPETH: There, there, my darling, there, there ...

JUSTIN: Mike, old man — I'm sorry ...

MIKE: I know, it's up to me now. It's ironical, isn't it? Suddenly I've got something to live for.

[*He gives an ironical laugh.*]

MAISIE: It takes a few old mountains to teach us the truth about ourselves. And somehow, when we face up to the truth, it stops being important any more.

ELSPETH: It's these mountains. They're wiser than any of us.

MIKE: I'll go then. I'll make it. I'm stronger than you, Justin, I've kept myself fit all these years, trained my body hard, tried to make a he-man of myself, to please my old dad. Ha! While deep down underneath —

MAISIE: Don't say it, Mike.

MIKE: Shut up, Maisie. You gotta know this before I — go out there. You gotta know who I really am, what I really am. You gotta know what I've been covering up all these years, when I was putting on the big all-American boy act . . .

JUSTIN: If you mean your CIA work, I know about that . . .

MIKE: Worse than that. Ah. Maisie, if only I'd met you ten years ago, you might have done something for me. Now it's too late.

MAISIE: It's never too late —

MIKE: Don't you understand what I'm telling you? That I'm rotten? A hollow sham? Well, I'll spell it out. Maisie, I'm queer! I'm a fruit, Maisie.

[*He sobs brokenly.*]

MAISIE: Why, you fool! Do you think I didn't know?

MIKE: You — knew?

MAISIE: Don't you understand, it makes no difference! I love you, Mike. Listen, we'll fight this thing, fight it together. And we'll win, Mike, we'll win. And now, go out there and find young Kurt. I'll be waiting for you. I love you. More than that. I — admire you, Mike.

MIKE: Shut up, Maisie . . . Well, I'll be seeing you.

[*He opens the door. Blizzard.*]

ILSE: No! You shall not go!

[*She shuts the door.*]

MIKE: Out of the way, Ilse! I gotta go!

ILSE: Stand back, I varn you!

[*She takes out a knife.*]

ELSPETH: Look out, she's got a knife! Keep away from her, Justin! She's mad!

JUSTIN: Give me that knife, Ilse. I said, give — me — that — knife!

ILSE: Keep beck, Englishman.

[*She stares at him, fighting him with her eyes and at the same time fighting within herself. She gives a broken, twisted smile.*]

So, I vas wrong. Wrong about you all. I took you to be veak, effete, despicable. Ach! I see now! All my life I have lived a lie. But I am not beaten yet. I go now. I shall prove that I, Ilse von Bahrendorfer, have still some Charman blood in my veins. Goodbye!

    [*She opens the door.* JUSTIN *grabs her.*]

JUSTIN: No you don't!

ELSPETH: Look out, Justin!

ILSE: Let me go! I must prove myself!

    [*They struggle.* JUSTIN *gives a cry of pain.*]

ELSPETH: Justin, you're hurt! Take that, you cow!

    [*She hits* ILSE *with her discarded snowboot.* ILSE *cries out and falls.*]

JUSTIN: Well done, Elspeth; that snowboot came in handy.

ELSPETH: Justin, you're bleeding.

JUSTIN: Just a scratch.

MAISIE: My God, Ilse. She's fallen on the knife. Horrible, horrible . . .

    [OLD KURT *gives a cry and begins to speak rapidly.*]

MIKE: What's he saying? Ilse, for God's sake, what's the old man saying??

ILSE: [*struggling to speak*] He say . . . zat ze avalanche . . . is coming. So . . . [*She gives a crooked laugh.*] Who vins . . . in ze end . . . and who . . . loses? [*She feebly raises one arm in salute.*] Heil — !

    [*With a cry* ILSE *passes out. The avalanche begins to be heard.* OLD KURT *takes charge of the situation, giving the others orders which they obey as best they can.*]

JUSTIN: Listen. It's coming.

ELSPETH: It's strange, Justin. I feel oddly calm. I'm not frightened any more. It's as if it all happened long, long ago, in some far distant place, to somebody else . . .

JUSTIN: We've done the best we can. We've all done the best we can.

MAISIE: May God forgive us all.

MIKE: Shut up, Maisie.

JUSTIN: Here it comes.

> [*Then the avalanche is upon them, tossing them hither and thither like so much matchwood. It passes.*]

Elspeth . . . Are you all right?

ELSPETH: I think so. Are you all right?

JUSTIN: I'm all right. All right, Mike?

MIKE: Sure, I'm all right. How are you, Maisie ? All right?

MAISIE: I'm all right, Mike.

ELSPETH: Look. Old Kurt . . .! Is he . . .?

> [OLD KURT *is slumped insensibly on the floor.* MIKE *examines him.*]

MIKE: He's gonna be all right.

ELSPETH: Thank God! Oh, thank God!

MAISIE: What happened? Why aren't we all dead? Perhaps we are! Perhaps we're all dead, and only imagining we're alive. That would be ironical, wouldn't it?

MIKE: Shut up, Maisie. Look. Out of the window.

JUSTIN: What can you see, Mike?

MIKE: The avalanche. It went down the other side of the mountain.

ELSPETH: So the mountain decided to spare us after all. She must think we are not quite worthless . . . [*She laughs.*] It's ironical.

JUSTIN: Or not worth bothering with.

> [*He laughs.*]

ELSPETH: And look! The sky's clearing! The snow's stopped. The wind has dropped! The sun is coming out! Justin, we're safe . . .

> [*She sobs.*]

MAISIE: You know, the funny thing about life is that all the old cliches are true.

MIKE: Well, Maisie, seems we're stuck with one another a while longer yet.

MAISIE: It seems we are, big boy . . . [*They kiss.*] Say, where did you learn to kiss like that? Don't tell me.

JUSTIN: And look! Look! Over there!

MIKE: What?

ELSPETH: What can you see?

JUSTIN: That struggling figure? Carrying our provisions? It's —

MIKE: It's not — ? Is it?

JUSTIN: It is! Young Kurt! Good old Young Kurt! He didn't run away after all! He went back to save the provisions!

YOUNG KURT: [*far distant cry*] Hullooo!

> [OLD KURT *emits a stream of Swiss German interspersed with sobs, while tears roll down his old face.*]

MIKE: That's it, cry, old man. Don't be afraid to cry. It's not the outside that makes a man, no, nor a woman neither. It's that thing deep down inside, that quality, that thing that keeps on, that keeps us going. That's what makes men and women of us.

JUSTIN: Mike . . .

MIKE: Justin . . .

> [*They shake hands.*]

ILSE: Ach, mein Gott . . .

ELSPETH: Ilse! Are you all right?

> [*She staggers to her feet.*]

ILSE: Ja. I am all right. I have been a stupid, blind fool. I vish to apologise.

JUSTIN: We all make mistakes, Ilse. Don't we, Elspeth, old girl?

ELSPETH: It's not too late, is it, Justin? I mean — for us?

JUSTIN: You mean — to start again?

ELSPETH: Shall we give it a try? I seem to have learnt so much.

JUSTIN: We'll give it a try. Come on, old girl, we'll go down the mountain together.

ELSPETH: Oh, what a beautiful day!

JUSTIN: Come, Ilse, we must get you to hospital.

ILSE: Ja. Vounds can turn nasty in ze mountains.

ELSPETH: Are you coming Mike?

MIKE: I'm coming . . . You coming, Maisie?

MAISIE: Sure, Mike, I'm coming. We've got a lot of living to do.

ILSE: Come, Old Kurt. Take my arm. Ve shall help each ozzer. Zat is ze vay ve shall survive. Come.

> [OLD KURT *agrees, in Swiss German. They make their way out of the hut and down towards* YOUNG KURT, *tears streaming down their faces.*]

THE END

BIRDSONG

Characters

TINKER
JOEY
TRIXIE

Birdsong was written for the Richmond Fringe and first performed by them at the Orange Tree Theatre, Richmond on 5 August, 1979. The cast was as follows:

TINKER	Clive Wouters
JOEY	David Gooderson
TRIXIE	Penelope Nice

It was directed by Hugh Walters.

A birdcage: in it a suspended mirror, a feeding trough, a swing, a seesaw, a hanging bell. The cage is being swept out. A bucket of bits of bread, etc, is tipped into the trough. The cleaner leaves. The cage door is heard to clang shut. After a while the door is heard to open; TINKER and JOEY tumble in. The door shuts.

TINKER: Here we are again. The start of another lovely day.
        [JOEY looks around, head jerking.]
JOEY: Spit and a lick they do nowadays.
        [He goes to the trough and takes a bit of bread.]
Hard as a rock. And I'll wager they haven't wiped the mirror.
        [TINKER is looking at himself in the mirror.]
TINKER: Pretty boy, pretty boy, pretty boy. Who's a pretty boy then?
        [He shadow-boxes with his reflection. He stops, and thinks, his head on one side.]
If you looked in a mirror . . . and didn't see anybody there . . . would you assume (a) you were invisible (b) the natural laws had gone on the blink (c) you were deluding yourself, or (d) . . .?
JOEY: I was a vampire.
TINKER: Yes.
JOEY: Are we starting already?
TINKER: At your convenience.
JOEY: Right. Since I don't believe in the impossible — Wait a minute . . .
TINKER: Go on.
JOEY: That's a tautology, it means nothing. The impossible is by definition unbelievable in.
TINKER: No it's not.
JOEY: Of course it is.
TINKER: No it's not. Not if you believe in the impossible.
JOEY: What?
TINKER: If you do believe in the impossible — and what's to stop you — it can't be.
        [JOEY stares at him for a moment.]
JOEY: You're right. I'm wrong. The impossible *isn't* un-

believable in ... It doesn't sound right. Where am I making my mistake?

TINKER: You want me to tell you?

JOEY: Yes.

TINKER: You assumed falsely that belief is rational. There's nothing to forbid irrational belief. You introduced the false assumption by giving a false definition of the word 'impossible', and moreover an imprecise definition. It was that imprecision which allowed the error, a common trick, I soon saw through that.

JOEY: Go on.

TINKER: You said the impossible is by definition unbelievable in. What do you mean by 'unbelievable in'?

JOEY: Not open to belief. In.

TINKER: By whom? By everyone? Or by one, meaning the generality? Or by you?

JOEY: Ah. Yes ... We're fishing in very treacherous waters here, you know.

TINKER: We are. But let's keep our heads. It'll help, I think, if we draw a distinction between what is or is not impossible, which concerns the phenomenal, and what is or is not the *meaning* of the *word* 'impossible', which is semantics. I take it we're dealing with semantics, that is, that for present purposes meaning and definition are synonymous. Fair?

JOEY: I'll accept that.

TINKER: Splendid. So what *is* your definition of the impossible?

JOEY: Ah, now, wait, you're saying *my* definition rather than *the* definition. Isn't that begging a question?

TINKER: *Your* definition of *the* definition, what's the difference?

JOEY: I don't know ...

TINKER: What is it, then? What everyone finds unbelievable in, what the generality finds unbelievable in, or what you personally find unbelievable in?

JOEY: Good Lord ... Everyone.

TINKER: Oh, come now.

JOEY: Ah! No! Yes, I see! You're saying that it needs only one individual to believe irrationally in the possibility of the impossible to render the definition invalid.

TINKER: You've hit it.

JOEY: The generality then. Oh, I'm enjoying this. The impossible is what most individuals find impossible; not possible; accept to be . . . not possible. It still sounds like a tautology.

TINKER: But it still leaves open the *possibility* of an irrational belief in the possibility of the impossible.

JOEY: Yes . . . Are we going round in circles here?

> [TINKER *squawks and takes a couple of swipes at the bell.*]

Let me try another tack. I'll grant you the fact that the statement: 'The impossible is by definition unbelievable in' is not necessarily true . . .

> [*He thinks.*]

TINKER: Come on, come on.

JOEY: Unless, wait a minute, *unless* the *definition* of the word 'definition' includes implicitly the rider: 'A definition is valid only for those who accept its validity, i.e. the generality, but is *still for them* valid if somewhere there is some idiot who doesn't.'

TINKER: What?

JOEY: Accept it.

TINKER: The definition of a definition.

JOEY: No, the definition.

TINKER: Ah.

JOEY: The said idiot then falls outside the *scope* of the definition; we, so to speak, wall it off from him. In this way, the problem of universality is solved not by an expansion of the definition to cover all possible cases but by constricting the universe to fit the definition. Then if someone does not find the impossible beyond belief, the impossible he does not find beyond belief is *his* impossible not ours, is in fact what we would call the possible; so that from our point of view —

TINKER: Yes, I take the point. Neat.

JOEY: I think Wittgenstein could have helped us here. We've been barking up the wrong creek.

TINKER: 'Confusions arise when language is like an engine idling, not when it is doing work.'

JOEY: I had in mind his thoughts on the indefiniteness of a definition.

TINKER: Imprecision is better.

JOEY: Right, the imprecise nature of a definition around its limits. Or even within them. Once that imprecision is accepted, one can speak of a definition being generally correct without having to define what one means by 'generally' or 'correct'. One can even speak of it as precisely true, so long as the definition of 'precisely' is allowed a certain imprecision. After all, how long *is* a metre?

TINKER: Exactly.

JOEY: Or not exactly.

TINKER: That's what I mean. Precisely. We must never forget Wittgenstein.

JOEY: You refer, of course, to Bert Wittgenstein the plumber.

TINKER: Exactly. And by 'we' I mean of course everyone except jackdaws and parakeets.

JOEY: And by 'never' you mean, naturally, until the 28th of August, 2012.

[TINKER *gives a cry of pleasure.* JOEY *answers it and gets off his seesaw.*]

I wonder if they've put any biscuits in the trough today. I just fancy a biscuit.

[*He roots around and picks up what might be a biscuit.*]

Is it a tautology to say that a biscuit is biscuit-shaped?

[*He takes a bite.*]

Is a biscuit with a bite out of it shaped like a biscuit or shaped like a bite? Or both or neither or something in between? Must a biscuit baked in the form of a row of teeth not still necessarily be in the shape of a biscuit since that is what it is, and should the twin indentations made by a vampire in the throat of his victim, ah! I was going to say: since *I*, with the rest of the generality, define the impossible as that which cannot happen, and since I put into that category any suspension of the natural laws, then I have to assume that I would not assume that the natural laws had gone on the blink, unless at the time I were suffering from delusions. By the same token I'd not assume I was invisible, and a brief glimpse at myself would confirm my visibility, at least to myself, I mean would confirm at least to myself my visibility to myself. That disposes of the invisibility hypothesis. Since I eat biscuits — bread — I am not a vampire. This leaves the assumption that I'm suffering a delusion.

TINKER: Ah ...

JOEY: I know what you're going to say. No-one can *know* they are deluding themselves, it's an error of the same order as knowing one doesn't exist. That leaves only one possibility: the whole bloody thing is impossible. You've set an unreal problem.

TINKER: Oh no I haven't.

JOEY: Oh yes you have.

TINKER: Oh no I haven't. If I run past the mirror fast enough I can get to the other side before the reflected light has time to hit me.

JOEY: You can't run faster than the speed of light.

TINKER: I could go into training.

JOEY: If you're going to be flippant —

TINKER: All right. I don't have to run faster than the speed of light. All I have to do is make the distance from me to the mirror and back greater than the distance I have to run and then run at something less than the speed of light, as in the Michelson-Morley experiments.

JOEY: Go on, then, do it.

TINKER: I don't feel like it.

JOEY: Because it's impossible.

TINKER: Not theoretically.

JOEY: Do it theoretically, then. Ah!

TINKER: Right you are.
> [*He positions himself.*]
> I'll do it both ways, there and back, to cancel out errors in the system. Are you watching? Say now.

JOEY: Now. Have you done it?

TINKER: Yes.

JOEY: That was quick.

TINKER: It has to be.

JOEY: Did it work?

TINKER: Oh yes. I'll do it again if you don't believe me. As soon as I get my breath back.

JOEY: There's no way I can prove you a liar, is there?

TINKER: No.

JOEY: Oh, I do enjoy our little flights.

TINKER: They are fun, aren't they?

JOEY: What shall we do now?

TINKER: Don't rush it. All the time in the world.

> [JOEY *goes to the trough and sorts through it.*]

JOEY: Pretty basic fodder this morning again. They're definitely cutting down, you know. We're not getting the biscuits like we used to. It used to be biscuits with bits of bread, now it's bread with bits of biscuit.

TINKER: Nothing wrong with bread.

JOEY: Oh no, no ...

> [TINKER *does a few exercises.*]

Pretty light on the cuttlefish too, lately, have you noticed?

TINKER: What's a cuttlefish more or less?

JOEY: A member of the genus *Sepia,* most commonly *Sepia officinalis.* More or less. And I'm partial to it. And we haven't had one for a week. It's not much to ask.

> [TINKER *begins a bit of improvised whistling.*]

As for the way they're cleaning up nowadays ...

TINKER: You don't know you're born, that's your trouble.

JOEY: I do, I do. I'm not complaining.

TINKER: Sounded like it to me.

JOEY: I wouldn't mind a bit of cuttlefish is all I'm saying.

TINKER: What do you think it's like out there, eh?

JOEY: I'm not talking about out there —

TINKER: You think there's biscuits for the asking? Cuttlefish hanging from every perch?

JOEY: I've no idea.

TINKER: You'd be lucky.

JOEY: As you know, I don't know a thing about out there. I've never been in a position to sample its delights.

TINKER: Oh, yes, delights, my word, ha ha.

JOEY: As you once did.

TINKER: Once is enough, believe me.

JOEY: Really bad, was it?

          [TINKER *doesn't answer.*]

          You've never told me anything about it . . . How long
          were you out for?

TINKER: It's not something I particularly want to talk about.

JOEY: Roughly. I mean was it weeks, or days or — hours?

TINKER: Weeks. I mean days.

JOEY: What do you mean, weeks you mean days?

TINKER: It seemed like weeks. It seemed like eternity. I began to
          believe in hell. Out there.

JOEY: What was it like?

TINKER: I've just told you. Hell. It was like hell.

          [*Pause.*]

JOEY: It's an interesting use of language, to say something is
          like hell. By general consent, I mean according to usage,
          hell is worse than anything on earth; hell is always like
          the worst you can imagine, only worse. So that to say
          that an actual experience was like hell is to say it was
          like the actual experience, only worse. Which is like
          saying —

TINKER: Oh, do shut up.

JOEY: Sorry.

TINKER: It was worse than you can imagine. That's why I call it
          hell.

JOEY: Yes . . .

          [*Pause.*]

          In other words, it was like *my* hell, since it carried the
          necessary connotation that it was worse than I could
          imagine, but it couldn't be like *your* hell, since having
          experienced it you must be able to imagine it; or remem-
          ber it, which is the same thing; I think. I mean remem-
          bering something is only like imagining something
          which, as it happens, has already happened . . . I mean if
          you *mis*remember something, which means you
          imagine something else than what actually happened,
          to you and anyone else who didn't know the actual
          course of events you'll be simply remembering . . . You

could say that imagining carries with it a creative component which remembering does not; but suppose I say 'I remember a bird with blue feathers', can that really be said to carry more of a creative component than the equally unremarkable statement 'I remember a bird with green feathers', even if the original bird had in fact green rather than blue feathers . . .? So that although *you* can tell *me* it was like hell, if *I'd* asked *you*, 'Do you think it was like hell?' you'd have to say, 'No, of course it wasn't, it couldn't possibly be . . .'

TINKER: I'm getting a little tired of this.

JOEY: Sorry.

[TINKER *begins to whistle.*]

I didn't know you were into twelve-note . . . I must say I prefer good old-fashioned chromaticism.

TINKER: You know what you like.

JOEY: *That* ought to be a tautology.

[*There is a whistling from another cage.*]

There's that friend of yours from down the row.

TINKER: He's no friend of mine.

JOEY: I thought he was.

[*The whistling comes again.* TINKER *answers it.*]

Ask if they've had any cuttlefish down there.

[TINKER *whistles and is replied to. They hold a brief conversation.*]

TINKER: Miserable bugger.

JOEY: What's he say?

TINKER: Terrible what's happened to him. How he's let himself go down.

JOEY: What's he say about cuttlefish?

TINKER: He hasn't looked. He says he's not opening his eyes this morning.

JOEY: Why not? Is he ill?

TINKER: He says he doesn't see any mileage in it.

JOEY: What's he mean by that?

TINKER: Ask him yourself.

JOEY: You know I haven't got the languages.

TINKER: He says he's seen it all before.

[*Another whistle.* TINKER *answers. Another whistle.*]

Oh, piss off if that's the way you feel . . . There's always one about. Trouble-maker, oddball. He doesn't know he's born.

[*A whistle, like a dirge.* TINKER *replies. No answer. He tries again. No answer.*]

Over and out.

JOEY: What was that about?

TINKER: I wouldn't repeat it . . .

[*A mynah bird starts up.*]

Wrap up, you! Go back to where you came from! Bloody mynah birds . . . I used to share a cage with him, you know.

JOEY: Him down the row?

TINKER: We were great mates at one time. We used to have some marvellous discussions. Modes of being, the meaning of meaning, really theoretical stuff, no rubbish. I was really upset when they moved me out. We carried on corresponding after I was put in here, but the joy seemed to go out of it for him. He started getting serious. He'd break off in the middle of a philosophical discussion to complain about the food.

[*He looks pointedly at* JOEY.]

When he began to go on about the quality of life I realised I had nothing more to say to him. He got really maudlin, I was getting to dread the sound of his whistle, it was getting me down. Then you arrived, and we hit it off together, and I decided he could get stuffed. I've hardly heard a peep from him lately, I don't think he can be bothered. Once you lose your positive attitude, you see, you're done for. It's a slippery slope, you don't last long.

[*Pause.*]

I'd hate to see you go the same way.

JOEY: What are you talking about? You're not comparing me with him, are you?

TINKER: Do you mind if I speak frankly?

JOEY: There's nothing wrong with a bit of a grumble now and

then. Better out than in.

TINKER: May I speak frankly?

JOEY: Go ahead.

TINKER: I have had a bit more experience than you, you know; inside and out. I don't want to pull pecking order . . .

JOEY: Go on, go on.

TINKER: As you say, there's nothing wrong with a bit of a grumble, a *bit* of a grumble, we all do it, it's a means of expression. The trouble comes when it begins to get habitual, when you begin to turn from the particular to the general, from 'Not many biscuits this morning' to 'Biscuits are becoming scarcer', from 'They've forgotten the cuttlefish today' to 'We don't get the cuttlefish we used to get in the old days'. And it's not much of a slide from there to 'The quality of life is deteriorating', to 'Life is not worth living any more', to 'I don't think I'll bother to open my eyes this morning, this week, ever again . . .' And that's when your feathers start dropping out, mate.

[*The bird call is heard again, like an elegy.*]
You hear that? I don't know what they're thinking of to leave him there; putting out stuff like that. The rest of us have to go on living if he doesn't.

JOEY: What did he say?

TINKER: I'm not going to translate . . . They ought to have a special unit . . .
[*Pause.*]

JOEY: How many days?

TINKER: What?

JOEY: Were you out?

TINKER: You're a bit obsessive about that, aren't you?

JOEY: I'm only asking. I'm interested.

TINKER: Well you needn't be. There's nothing to be interested about. It's boring out there. It's a dull, boring hell.

JOEY: Four? Five . . .? One?

TINKER: Two.

JOEY: Only two . . .

TINKER: What do you mean, only two?

JOEY: I just had the impression you were out longer than that. From the way you used to go on about it.

TINKER: I never have gone on about it. You're the one who's going on about it.

JOEY: I mean how you used to go on about not being able to talk about it.

TINKER: It's not that I'm not able to, it's that I don't want to, it's boring, it bores me.

JOEY: And about what a traumatic experience and so on.

TINKER: Well, it was.

JOEY: I can see it was ... I don't quite see how it could be traumatic *and* boring ...

TINKER: You put yourself in a totally boring situation for days on end and see if it's not traumatic ... And cold, and lonely, and ...

JOEY: Sometimes it's better to talk about these things, you know, bring them into the open. Any psychiatrist will tell you. Rather than let them fester inside ...

TINKER: It's not festering.

JOEY: No ...

TINKER: And sometimes it's a good thing to respect someone's wishes if, for some reason, like finding a subject boring, he doesn't want to keep going on about it.

JOEY: Hm ...

TINKER: You think two days wasn't enough?

JOEY: It obviously was. More than enough.

> [*Pause.* TINKER *attempts a cheerful whistle, but gives up.*]

TINKER: You've ruined the atmosphere now. Same as you did yesterday ...

> [*The birdcall starts up, mournful.*]

Put a bloody sock in it! Put a cloth over his cage, someone! Defeatism ... You're off-colour, aren't you?

JOEY: I don't think so.

TINKER: I think you are. You have been for some time. You eat too much, you don't get enough exercise. You're letting yourself go. It's a slippery slope, you know. Take my word for it, I've seen it happen. We're a lucky couple of buggers.

JOEY: In what way?

TINKER: In what way, in every way. Don't you think so?

JOEY: I suppose we are.

TINKER: No doubt about it. Can you think of anywhere else you'd rather be?

JOEY: I don't know anywhere else.

TINKER: Then what is it you want?

JOEY: Nothing, nothing . . .

TINKER: Think of it: every morning they clean out your cage, provide us with all the necessaries, and what do they ask in return? Nothing. They must be mad. We've got the whole of our lives, we're free to do as we like. Can you think of a better way to live?

JOEY: I don't know any other way to live. I've never lived any other way. Better or worse.

TINKER: I tell you, we're in clover. Take my word for it. Think positive, look on the bright side, count your blessings.
[*Pause.* JOEY *scratches his beak.*]

JOEY: Sorry I upset you.

TINKER: Upset me? Not at all. You're getting much too serious. It's a great life, it's a great life. No offence?

JOEY: No offence.
[*They take up the call together.*]

BOTH: No offence, no offence, no offence . . .!
[*They get into this, hopping about, screeching, bashing the bell. An answering chorus from elsewhere.*]

JOEY: We do have fun, don't we?

TINKER: We do all right. That's given me an appetite.
[TINKER *goes to the trough and roots around.*]

JOEY: Intellectual conversation, mirrors, bells . . .
[*He bashes the bell and gives a squawk of high spirits.*]

TINKER: And if we don't find a biscuit today —

BOTH: We may find a biscuit tomorrow!
[*They squawk.* TINKER *perches to eat his bit of bread.* JOEY *looks from place to place for something to fix his attention on, his head jerking quickly from one position to the next. Pause.*]

JOEY: 'I know what I like' is a tautology.
[*Pause.*]
Or: 'I don't know what I like' is a contradiction in

terms. There's a lot of mileage there. What do you think? The meaning of 'to like'; can 'I' be plural and if not how can I think about myself? Sadomasochism: can it be said that a masochist likes what he doesn't like, and is this the same as to say that he doesn't like what he does like? Is a sadist who gives a masochist what he doesn't like, i.e. what he likes, still a sadist . . .? What is it to know? Can one know what isn't true? It could take us right into psychoanalysis, the ego and the id, not forgetting the star of the show, the superego or double-yoked ego . . . What is the I that knows what which I likes? What do you think?

> [*There is a noise outside: a squawking, a cage door opening.*]

TINKER: Hello.

> [TRIXIE *is injected into the cage as if brought in by an enormous hand. The cage door shuts.*]

We have a visitor.

> [TRIXIE *sits on the floor where she has been put. The other two look at her with interest.*]

Always the possibility of the unexpected, you see. And hey hey hey, it's the opposite sex.

JOEY: As opposite as could be, I'd say.

TINKER: *Droit de seigneur* here, my lad. Remember the pecking order.

JOEY: And I was complaining of a shortage of biscuits.

> [TRIXIE *charges at the door. She falls back.*]

TINKER: I wouldn't do that if I were you . . .

TRIXIE: Bastards . . .

TINKER: Oh, come now, madam —

TRIXIE: Don't madam me!

TINKER: Oh dear, oh dear. One of those.

TRIXIE: Let me out you bastards!

> [*Her cry sets off a chorus of bird noises.* TINKER *and* JOEY *exchange glances.*]

TINKER: Welcome to our little nest. May I say on behalf of us both —

TRIXIE: Drop dead.

> [*Pause.*]

JOEY: I think perhaps the first step has to be an examination of whether there's any real difference between 'I like something' and 'I know that I like something'. One says immediately: *Any* statement predicates knowledge, or the statement could not be made. At the unconscious, that is the unthought unspoken level, the liking and the knowledge of liking are, as it were, of the same substance. It is only when the *concept* of liking comes into existence that knowledge appears, as it were, as a thing in itself. To state the concept is to state knowledge of it, the two are inseparable. But this being so, knowledge of this must also be, as it were, built into the statement of the concept. Thus to say 'I like something' is to say 'This is so'. It is also to say 'I know that this is so'. It is also to say 'I am telling you that I know that this is so, in other words I am aware of my knowledge'. And so on. Thus we find ourselves in a peculiar position. It seems that the carrying into consciousness of a concept as simple and factual as 'I like cuttlefish' produces of necessity and, as it were, at a stroke, an engagement with the processes of knowing, causing the original concept 'Cuttlefish is liked by me' to recede, as it were, further and further into the distance as if viewed through a succession of mirrors. There is obviously a flaw here . . .

> [*Meanwhile* TRIXIE *gets up. She goes towards the other two and stands looking at them, first one then the other.* JOEY *stops as she stands close, staring at him.*]

TINKER: I think we're in danger of falling into a semantic trap. As Wittgenstein said —

TRIXIE: You can stop that shit.

> [JOEY *crosses nonchalantly away from her to the trough.*]

JOEY: There might just be a bit of biscuit in amongst there.

> [*He roots around, but his attention is still on* TRIXIE. *She walks round the cage, casing it. She reaches the trough.*]

Have you had breakfast?

> [*He smiles and offers her a bit of bread. She*

knocks it out of his hand. He clears his throat.
She glares at them, one after the other.]

TRIXIE: A couple of institutionalised deadbeats. Out of the frying pan into the shit. Wouldn't you know . . .? Let me out of here!

[*An answering chorus from outside.* TINKER *winces.*]

Do you call yourself birds?

JOEY: Erm . . .

[*He looks questioningly at* TINKER.]

TINKER: Now look here —

TRIXIE: What are you called?

JOEY: Birds . . .?

TRIXIE: Your names.

JOEY: I'm, er, Joey; he's Tinker.

TRIXIE: What else . . .?

JOEY: Nothing else.

TINKER: Look, erm . . .

TRIXIE: You can call me Trixie.

JOEY: Nice name.

TRIXIE: Quit that.

TINKER: Look, Trixie, I think we've all got off on the wrong foot here.

[*She turns her gaze on him.*]

I know it's an unsettling experience to be suddenly moved from the place you've made your own into a strange cage; having to refamiliarise yourself, make new friends — as I sincerely hope we shall be before very long — settle into the new home. It's an experience I've not had to go through for some long time now, thank God, but I do remember very vividly the — traumatic effect it had on me. So much so that I quite lost my head, as a matter of fact, and did something rather foolish which I later bitterly regretted . . .

JOEY: Was that when you got out?

[TINKER *glares at him.*]

TINKER: But it did perhaps have one beneficial effect; I am, I think I can say without vanity, a little wiser as well as older than I was then; after that experience I've learnt to count my blessings, so that in a case like this, meeting someone in the same predicament that I was in then, I hope I can be of some little help in smoothing the way for you, making the transition less painful for you than it might otherwise ... be ... And I think you'll find when you get used to things that you've fallen in with not a bad couple of cagemates in a not bad little pad ... erm ...

TRIXIE: What's the matter with you, verbal bloody diarrhoea?

TINKER: I beg your pardon?

JOEY: I think what he's trying to say —

TRIXIE: Don't you start.

TINKER: I do think that given the unalterable facts of the matter a constructive attitude is the —

TRIXIE: Constructive attitude my tail.

TINKER: We've got a tough nut here.

TRIXIE: Let me out, you bastards!

TINKER: Stop that.

TRIXIE: Stop me.

[*She tips over the trough. Pause.*]

JOEY: Tinker ... I don't feel well ...

TINKER: You're upsetting my friend. He's not used to this kind of thing.

TRIXIE: Then he'd better *get* used to it. You too. Because this is the way it's going to be till they let me out of here.

TINKER: But what's wrong with it?

TRIXIE: It's a cage, isn't it?

TINKER: Of course it's a cage, it's a very pleasant cage. You won't find a better.

TRIXIE: I don't think you understand me yet. You said I'm a tough nut, I am. And I'm a stayer. I'm not one of your dilettantes, it's no hobby with me, it's a life's work. I don't give up. I wasn't long out of the egg when I set my sights on it, and I shall stick with it till I get it or till I die. Bastards!

[*This last not to them but to the world at large. She sits in the corner of the cage and broods. TINKER and JOEY exchange glances. JOEY raises his eyebrows questioningly. TINKER shrugs his shoulders. Pause.*]

JOEY: With what?
          [*No response from* TRIXIE.]
          Excuse me.
          [*She looks up.*]
          I didn't quite catch what it is you're talking about.
TRIXIE: Just out of reach, always just out of reach . . .
JOEY: Cuttlefish . . .?
TRIXIE: We're born without it, we live without it, we die
          without it.
                    [JOEY *crosses to* TINKER. *They confer quietly*
                    like members of a quiz panel.]
JOEY: Can you give us the first letter.
TRIXIE: Take the piss, I'm used to it.
JOEY: No, honestly.
TRIXIE: *I want freedom!* What the hell do you think I'm talking
          about?
TINKER: Freedom?
JOEY: You *want* it?
TINKER: I'm sorry, I don't quite understand your difficulty . . .
TRIXIE: Oh my God . . . They've put me in the psychiatric wing
          . . .
JOEY: No . . .
TRIXIE: You can tell me. This is the psychiatric wing, they've
          put me in the psychiatric wing, haven't they . . .?
          They've locked me up with a couple of screwballs,
          haven't they! Let me out you fuckers!
                    [*She makes a rush for the cage, bounces back.*]
TINKER: Oh dear, oh dear, oh dear . . .
JOEY: I don't like this, Tink . . .
                    [TINKER *decides to play therapist.*]
TINKER: Tell me, Trixie . . . How long have you felt like this?
TRIXIE: Don't give me that therapeutic shit!
                    [TINKER *sighs.*]
JOEY: What are we going to do, Tink?
TINKER: I think we've hit a classic case of semantic confusion
          here, Joey.
JOEY: You mean she —? No, I don't understand. What does
          she *want*?
                    [TINKER *spreads his hands.*]
TINKER: Freedom.

JOEY: She *wants* it? Where does she think she's going to *get* it from?

        [TRIXIE *puts her head in her wing.*]

TRIXIE: Oh God, oh God, oh God . . .

JOEY: Oh *God?*

        [TINKER *goes to* TRIXIE.]

TINKER: I'm sorry . . .

TRIXIE: I don't give a shit if you're sorry or not, leave me alone.

TINKER: No, I'm sorry, I didn't mean I was sorry. You know, this comes of living too long in the same company. One dwells more and more in the substratum of the language, that kind of alluvial deposit in which we burrow happily together, so to speak, making it our accustomed habitat, until a strange creature, taking up residence — No, the metaphor's not a good one. Look, I'm sorry. You want — freedom.

TRIXIE: Oh God, oh God . . .

TINKER: Now I want you to pay very close attention because I *think* we can straighten this thing out. You want freedom, now — Let's split that statement into two parts. There is you, with a — a want; and there's something which you are considering as separate from yourself — necessarily, since to think you want it implies that you think you don't have it. Well, I know one can talk of wanting what one already has, as 'I want *this* cuttlefish'. But I don't think that was your meaning, correct me if I'm wrong. So, there is you, there, yearning for what you call freedom, and there is, somewhere outside yourself — you assume — this — what? — thing, commodity, not a quality or condition certainly, if it stands on its own it must be clothed in its own form . . .

JOEY: I'm not sure about that.

TINKER: What?

JOEY: I admit one can't say 'I want green' or 'I want long', one can only say 'I want a green feather', or 'I want a long — cuttlefish'. On the other hand, one can say, surely, for instance, 'I want nobility'.

TINKER: But this is my point, Joey. The nobility one wants does not stand outside oneself. It exists, if it can be said to

exist before one has it, as a potential within oneself or as
a . . .

JOEY: Concept.

TINKER: A concept, exactly. And the concept of course is one's
own. The concept of freedom is one's own concept.
Which one already has. Now the question arises: in
what sense can freedom be more than a concept? And
what is it, if it is more than a concept? Because if it is *not*
more than a concept, and I don't see how it can be, as
soon as one *wants* it, one already *has* it . . .

> [*They have forgotten* TRIXIE *and are arguing
> between themselves.*]

TRIXIE: You dilettante shits!

> [*They look around.*]

I don't want to talk about fucking freedom, I want to
have it! I want to live it! I want to be it! Now! I want it!

> [TINKER *and* JOEY *exchange a glance.*]

JOEY: Want to *be* it . . .?

TRIXIE: I can't stand it any more. I'm a free creature, I want out
. . .

JOEY: You want . . .?

TRIXIE: Out! I want to get out!

> [*This interests* JOEY *and* TINKER.]

JOEY: You want to get *out*? As well?

TINKER: Out there?

TRIXIE: Where the hell else is out!

JOEY: My word . . .

TINKER: But it's nasty out there, Trixie.

TRIXIE: It's not! It's beautiful!

> [TINKER *shakes his head sadly.*]

It's marvellous, it's — big, not big, big's not big
enough, it's enormous, there's no end to it, it's a cage
with no bars, you can fly up, on up, past the perches, up
past everything, up till your wings get tired and your
breath gets short and there's still no top, no bars, you
can still fly on up and there's nothing, nothing . . . It's
. . . It's freedom . . .

> [JOEY *has become more and more disturbed by
> this speech. He shudders. Pause.*]

TINKER: I *see* ... You want ... outside; you want freedom. Freedom is outside, outside is freedom ... Hm ...

    [*The therapist has just had an insight into the patient's condition.*]

JOEY: Make her go away, Tinker.

TINKER: Have you been out there?

    [TRIXIE *shakes her head.*]

JOEY: He has.

TINKER: I have; for my sins.

    [*He looks sorrowfully at her.*]

    Oh Trixie. Oh, Trixie ...

    [*There is a whistle from the cage down the row.* TINKER *listens.*]

    Strange ...

    [TINKER *answers. They have a short conversation; or rather, the other bird takes off on a paean, a triumphant warble of joy, with interjections by* TINKER.]

    And bless you too, mate. Well, I suppose it's one way out for him, poor fellow ...

JOEY: What's happened?

TINKER: He's found God ... Or God's found him, he wasn't too coherent.

TRIXIE: He's what?

TINKER: Happy as a lark he is ... Whatever *that* is. Says he doesn't need a thing now God's with him. One way to deal with a shortage of cuttlefish, eh, Joe?

TRIXIE: After all I told him; after all the work I put in. Ah well, you win one, you lose one.

TINKER: You mean you were in there with him?

TRIXIE: For a while. They move me around. They don't know what to do with me, you see, I'm a disruptive influence. They put me in a cage with some songbird, it doesn't take long before he stops singing, his feathers start falling ... One day they'll let me go.

TINKER: You think so?

TRIXIE: Sure. They don't want my kind. They want the deadbeats, the songsters. Shit to that. I don't sing for their pleasure. They'll throw me out. You know what I've left

wherever I've been? A trail of discontented hearts.
That's good. And you know what I'll do when they let
me go?

TINKER: Fly up into the great big nothing?

TRIXIE: Sure, I'll fly up; I'll taste freedom, drink it, let it soak
into my bones and heart. And then I'll come back. I'll
perch outside, where they just can't reach me. *Then* I'll
sing. A real song, a song of freedom, a song of revolu-
tion. I'll sing, what are you doing in there, you shits?
This is life out here, this is real. Come out and get
living! I'll drive you all crazy.

> [TINKER *and* JOEY *exchange glances.*]

JOEY: Make her go away, Tink . . .

> [*Carried away by her rhetoric,* TRIXIE *begins a*
> *rhythmic chant, beating on the bell mean-*
> *while.*]

TRIXIE: Freedom! Freedom! Freedom! Liberty or death! Liberty
or death! Liberty or death! Freedom! Freedom!
Freedom!

> [*There is an answering uproar from the other*
> *cages.*]

JOEY: Tink . . .

TINKER: Joe?

JOEY: I think I'm developing one of my headaches . . . Tink . . .

> [JOEY *perches, his head covered by his wings.*
> TINKER *looks at him, then at* TRIXIE.]

TRIXIE: I want out! I want out! I want out, out, out! Liberty or
death! Liberty or death!

TINKER: I'm sorry . . .

> [*He goes over to her.*]

Excuse me; I'm sorry . . .

> [*She breaks off chanting but still beats the bell*
> *in a slow rhythm.*]

I underestimated you. I didn't realise how serious this is
to you. You must be free, mustn't you, you must be set
free.

TRIXIE: Shit to talk. Liberty or death! Liberty —!

TINKER: Not talk, a plan. I have a plan. To get you out. A
practical plan.

[*She looks at him suspiciously.*]

You don't believe me. You don't trust me. Understandable. Let me put my cards on the table ... I could explain better if you stopped ringing that bell for a moment.

[*She stops.*]

You are upsetting my friend, you see. I don't want that. Understand, my motives are purely selfish. As you've gathered, we are nothing more than a pair of institutionalised — twitterers. Songsters. As you put it, deadbeats. Our cage provides us with a feeling of comfort, security, relative well-being, which I know you find despicable. This is what we are. We pass the time, this is our highest ambition. Not much nobility in that, I know. We fly our few feet, now and then; the thought of more makes us uneasy. Birds with a fear of heights, it's quite ridiculous. But there you are. I did, as I told you, on one occasion sample the outside; what you call freedom; and found it, personally, insupportable ... I tell you all this merely to indicate that we have sufficient motive to not want you here, if I may so put it. You disturb us; you disturb my friend, and I need my friend. We'd like you to go away. Am I being honest?

[*She nods.*]

So that if I can think of a plan to offer you a chance to escape, just a bare chance, then you can understand that I'm willing for purely ignoble reasons to help you carry it out.

TRIXIE: Go on.

TINKER: You say they dislike you. You don't sing, you're a disruptive influence. They like us, though. We sing, we are model cage birds. Aren't we, Joey?

[JOEY *nods.*]

Now, suppose an argument develops, a fight. One of us falls, seems damaged, you lie apparently insensible, or dead, by the cage door ... They'd come, wouldn't they, to protect their songbirds; open the door, reach in to rescue me as I stand, squawking forlornly, nursing a damaged wing ...?

TRIXIE: And away I go.

TINKER: And away you go.

> [*Pause.*]

TRIXIE: Or they reach in for me.

TINKER: Possibly. One can't be sure. Without trying.

> [*Pause.*]

TRIXIE: Well, what are we waiting for? What's to lose?

TINKER: Exactly. Come along, Joey. Now, Trixie, I think if you stand there, so that you can fall just beside the door there. I stand here, so ... Joey!

JOEY: I don't like violence, Tinker, you know that.

TINKER: Come along, it's only a game! Only we have to make it look real. Stand behind Trixie, Joey. Now hold her ... No, really, really hold her ... That's it, I think we're ready. Trixie, I told you this was a purely selfish act on my part. I'm not sure that's entirely true. I should like to think you assumed there to be a small feeling of compassion as well. As a minor component.

TRIXIE: Yes, right, let's get going.

TINKER: Yes. When I say now, let's start squawking ... Now!

> [*They begin squawking.* TRIXIE *falls,* TINKER *on top of her, his hands round her neck.* TRIXIE *stops squawking.* TINKER *stops squawking.*]

You can stop now.

> [JOEY *stops squawking.* TINKER *and* JOEY *get up.* TRIXIE *stays still.* TINKER *rubs his wing.*]

I think I've sprained my wing ...

> [JOEY *is confused. He looks at* TINKER, *at* TRIXIE, *at* TINKER *again.*]

She did say liberty or death ... She'd have hated it out there ... It's cold; and open ... There's no bread, no cuttlefish. You look up and there's nothing, it's open, there's no top to it. You find a corner to get in, you crouch in the corner. You think: nobody knows I'm here, nobody will help me. Outside, enormous birds, with raucous voices, rapacious eyes, tearing beaks ... They wheel about, looking for something to tear. It's all open ... They'll take her away in a minute.

> [*He leads* JOEY *away from* TRIXIE. JOEY *gives a squawk.*]

No offence.
      [JOEY *squawks.*]
No offence.
      [TINKER *squawks.*]
JOEY: No offence.
BOTH: No offence! No offence! No offence . . .!
      [*There is an answering chorus.*]

THE END

POOR OLD SIMON

Characters

FATHER
MOTHER

Poor Old Simon was first performed as part of an entertainment *"Mixed Blessings"* at the Capitol Theatre, Horsham in 1973. The cast was as follows:

FATHER	Oscar Quitak
MOTHER	Andree Melly

It was subsequently presented by the Richmond Fringe at the Orange Tree Theatre on 16 April, 1976, with the following cast:

FATHER	James Greene
MOTHER	Ruth Goring

Both productions were directed by Sam Walters.

Half a String Quartet. The FATHER *sits clutching his violin like a club. The* MOTHER *is astride her cello. Chairs and music stands are arranged for the other two instruments, but the second violin's chair lies on its back, the violin beside it, and of the viola there is no sign. Both* MOTHER *and* FATHER *are looking toward the door, which has just slammed. After a moment, the* FATHER *turns to look for a moment at the* MOTHER.

FATHER: What was all that about?

MOTHER: You've upset her.

FATHER: I don't know what *she's* got to cry about. We're the losers. She obviously doesn't give a damn for the music.

MOTHER: That's not true.
        [*He plucks at a string and tunes it by ear.*]
        For a sensitive musician you can be surprisingly brash. Perfect pitch obviously isn't everything.
        [*He gets up and goes toward the door.*]
        Are you going to hit her with it?

FATHER: I thought I might go and ...

MOTHER: Leave her alone. She's perfectly all right. She only cried to stop you getting at her. It's the only way she knows —

FATHER: Getting at her? I wasn't getting at her.
        [*His eye lights on the discarded violin. He darts to pick it up. He examines it carefully, rubs the wood with his finger.*]
        She's scratched it. If you want my definition of brash, it's throwing an expensive violin on the floor.
        [*He plucks a string.*]
        No great damage.
        [*He tunes a string, comparing it with his own.*]

MOTHER: Tuning her violin won't put matters right.

FATHER: That wasn't my intention.
        [*He rights the chair, puts the violin on it, and sits in his own chair.*]
        It's so unnecessary. Why does *he* have to leave the quartet just because *she's* tired of him?

MOTHER: It's not that she's tired of him.

FATHER: Well, whatever it is. It seems to me rather a dog in the manger attitude: *she* doesn't want him, but she won't let *us* have him. I suppose we shall never see him again now.

MOTHER: I suppose not.

FATHER: He'll join the legion of the lost. Another scalp for her bedroom wall.

MOTHER: She doesn't enjoy it, you know.

FATHER: I'm not so sure about that. She's like that cat, bringing birds into the kitchen and then killing them behind the boiler.

MOTHER: Oh, really . . .

FATHER: Three times she's done it now.

MOTHER: Three?

FATHER: First Steve, then Mike, and now Simon.

MOTHER: You can't count Steve.

FATHER: Why not?

MOTHER: He only lasted three weeks.

FATHER: She brought him in, didn't she? We met him, we got to know him.

MOTHER: Well, hardly.

FATHER: I was getting to know him very well. We had that long talk together about the free schools. He was an interesting lad, very bright, I enjoyed talking to him. A fresh young mind. I was very cut up about it when she threw him over. Why does she do it? I wouldn't mind if she'd bring in a really unpleasant one, somebody I couldn't bear the sight of. It'd be a relief. But these were nice lads, all three of them. That's what I don't understand: she obviously has the ability to attract really nice lads, and then she throws them all away. It's such a waste.

MOTHER: She's as sorry about it as we are.

FATHER: Then why does she do it?

MOTHER: They want to sleep with her, that's why.

FATHER: That's natural enough. What's wrong with that?

MOTHER: Nothing, only she doesn't want to sleep with them.

FATHER: Why not?

MOTHER: *I* don't know.

FATHER: Not any one of them?

MOTHER: No.

FATHER: I don't understand. They were nice lads —

MOTHER: I *know* they were. That's not the point. And it's not really our business to understand why our daughter should want or not want to go to bed with a particular person.

FATHER: Look, explain to me, you're a woman. She liked all three of them, yes? Steve, Mike and Simon. She liked their company, as we did, she brought them home, at least one of them was a very good musician —

MOTHER: That's got nothing to do with it.

FATHER: No. All right. Though I wish she'd made it clear at the outset that how long he'd be playing with us would be dependent on her sexual whims. And they were all good-looking lads. Personable, good-looking — sexy lads.

MOTHER: I don't see that we can —

FATHER: Well, weren't they?

MOTHER: *I* thought so, yes.

FATHER: So did I. Well, then, why won't she sleep with them?

MOTHER: Whether, darling, *I* find them sexy or *you* find them sexy is not the point —

FATHER: I didn't say I found them sexy. Well, yes, theoretically I find — What I mean is, as you very well know, that I can see that they are, can be, sexually attractive lads. Young men.

MOTHER: But not necessarily to her. And even if they are —

FATHER: Then what does she *want*? I mean, how many — ? What kind of an Adonis is she saving herself for, for Christ's sake?

MOTHER: There's nothing wrong with her.

FATHER: I'm not saying there is.

MOTHER: She has slept with people.

FATHER: Has she?

MOTHER: Of course she has. She slept with Mike as a matter of fact.

FATHER: I'm glad to hear it. When?

MOTHER: What do you mean, when? When she knew him.

FATHER: Here?

MOTHER: How should I know?

FATHER: He stayed the night here a couple of times.

MOTHER: Well, then, it may have happened here. What does it matter?

FATHER: It doesn't. I just wondered how you know.

MOTHER: She told me, of course.

FATHER: She didn't tell me.

MOTHER: Why should she tell you?

FATHER: She told you. So what happened with Mike?

MOTHER: That *was* Mike.

FATHER: I mean why did she give him up?

MOTHER: Oh. Well, because she stopped wanting to sleep with him.

FATHER: Why, what's the matter with him?

MOTHER: Nothing, as far as I know.

FATHER: Then what's the matter with her?

MOTHER: What is it you want of our daughter?

FATHER: I don't want anything, I'm just —

MOTHER: Do you want her to have casual sexual relationships, or do you want her to have profound and meaningful sexual relationships?

FATHER: What a question. I don't know. Both.

MOTHER: Well then, she has had casual sexual relationships, and for some reason they no longer at the moment suit her, so she's temporarily more or less given up sexual relationships until she finds someone she can have a — what she thinks is a, profound one with.

FATHER: I wonder what the difference is.
[*She gives him a glance.*]
What do you mean by 'temporarily more or less given up'?

MOTHER: I only know what she tells me. I don't pry into her business.

FATHER: But Mike wasn't casual.

MOTHER: He was fairly casual.

FATHER: He was a good friend. They got on very well together.

MOTHER: *You* got on very well together.

FATHER: We all did. We all liked each other very much.

MOTHER: Yes, I know, it was very cosy. But to her, it was casual. In fact, she says, it was only after she started sleeping with him that she realised how casual it was. That's why she stopped. Because she didn't want to have a casual sexual affair with someone on a regular basis.

FATHER: Oh.

MOTHER: Especially since he didn't find it casual.

FATHER: Ah. So what about Steve?

MOTHER: She didn't sleep with Steve.

FATHER: Why not? She slept with Mike. What's wrong with Steve?

MOTHER: She hadn't started when she knew Steve.

FATHER: But he wanted to.

MOTHER: Yes, that's why she had to give him up.

FATHER: And found Mike. And then she did with Mike.

MOTHER: Yes.

FATHER: And Simon?

MOTHER: No.

FATHER: Why not?

MOTHER: I've just told you.

FATHER: Right. I've got it. Steve was in her virginal period, hard luck, Steve. Mike was in her casual period, so she did, but then she went profound, and stopped, hard luck, Mike. And Simon was in her profound period, but as far as she was concerned he was casual, so she didn't, hard luck, Simon. Is that right?

MOTHER: Absolutely. Do you understand now?

FATHER: I'm completely bemused. What bloody heavy weather to make of a simple biological function. Thank God she doesn't apply the same reasoning to what she eats or she'd starve to death. What's she trying to do, get into the *Guinness Book of Records*?

MOTHER: I don't know what you mean. Anyway, she has to conduct her emotional life her own way. It's none of our business.

FATHER: And meanwhile she wrecks our quartet.

MOTHER: That's rather a selfish way of looking at it.

FATHER: Not at all; she's the selfish one. Why shouldn't he carry on playing with us? It's only once a week. Viola players don't grow on trees. Not good ones like Simon. We were coming along really nicely, there was an empathy there, especially between me and him. Did you notice that?

MOTHER: Mm ...

FATHER: He liked coming here, old Simon; and it was doing his technique a world of good. But I suppose if she's going to make it a condition of membership that they have to have a profound sexual relationship with her ...

MOTHER: You're being unfair again. Anyway, she brought him in, he's her friend, so there's nothing we can do.

FATHER: But he's not, is he? Her friend. She's given him up. Now he's our friend. We haven't given him up. What does she want to do, sell him to somebody else? He's not her property; he's a person, not a cricket bat.

MOTHER: Well, all right. But if *he's* decided not to come —

FATHER: Who said he's decided?

MOTHER: She did. She said they'd both decided it was best that he doesn't come any more.

FATHER: Yes, I know. She said the same thing about Mike. He was hanging about outside all the evening, ringing her up from the corner phone box.

MOTHER: Well, you know how it is. Anyway, you can't put it all onto her. They're old enough to be responsible for themselves. If Simon had wanted to carry on coming here she couldn't have stopped him, he's free.

FATHER: Rubbish. As far as we're concerned he is, not as far as she's concerned. She gets them by the short and curlies, she plays the old territory game. The territory and property game. *Her* house, *her* family, *her* quartet. I can just hear her doing it. This is what really saddens me, you know: how reactionary the new generation can still be. She talks about the alternative society, but what she's really hooked on is territory and property, same as ever. She's worse than we were; at least she's got the opportunity, she lives in a permissive environment. Well, I suppose it's bound to be a slow process, deconditioning our society. Perhaps *her* children will be a bit more liberated.

[*He plucks a string.*]

I wish to God *I'd* been born eighteen years ago. To parents like us. Ha ha, I wouldn't be making heavy weather of it. My God . . .

MOTHER: If it really was such a permissive society, you'd permit her to live it her own way not keep criticising her for not being permissive enough.

FATHER: I don't criticise her, I'm very careful not to. I've never criticised anything she's done.

MOTHER: No, only the things she doesn't do.

FATHER: Not to her I don't.

MOTHER: The things she stops doing. You don't criticise her choice of friends, you just make her life a misery when she decides to give one of them up. It's just as bad.

FATHER: Three of them up.

MOTHER: You know what it is, of course.

FATHER: What?

MOTHER: What it is, you're trying to live your life again through her; it's a very common thing. Just because you had a frustrated adolescence —

FATHER: I did not!

MOTHER: — which you blame on your parents, you think it's her duty to make up for all you lost. By being free to behave as you want her to. And, of course, at the same time, you identify with her boyfriends, who want their oats like you did and can't get them. Like you couldn't. Only if you found they *were* getting them you'd be secretly jealous of her and envious of them. So you make sure you're in on it by trying to be more friendly with her friends than she is.

FATHER: Absolute rubbish. What have you been reading? You like them too.

MOTHER: Yes, I know.

FATHER: I need young company. It refreshes me. Where else will I find it if not through her? A parent should be able to communicate with his daughter's friends. I don't want to be like my parents were, I never dared take anyone home. I want her to — feel free to . . . If she doesn't want us to make friends with them she'd better stop bringing them home, that's all I can say. Poor old

Mike, he had a bad time. I liked him, though he was tone-deaf. Though I think I liked Simon best of the lot, didn't you?

MOTHER: I was very fond of all three of them. But it's their life, you see.

FATHER: And ours.

MOTHER: And they'll still have their problems to sort out, however much freedom you think you're giving them. Some people will still want their oats, and other people will still not. You know how it is.

FATHER: Wait a minute.

> [*He thinks.*]

Yes.

MOTHER: Shall we try a duo?

FATHER: No, I'm not in the mood. Listen: we've got Simon's number, haven't we?

MOTHER: Yes, it's in the book.

FATHER: Why don't we give him a ring?

MOTHER: We can't do that.

FATHER: Why not? Poor old Simon, you know he liked dropping in on us. We could just mention that *if* he ever wants to drop by . . . I mean, to see us, or to bring his viola along . . .

MOTHER: What, on a casual basis, you mean?

FATHER: Yes. On a purely casual basis. Just a general invitation to drop in when he feels like it. No pressure either way. What do you think?

MOTHER: I don't know what she'd say about it . . .

FATHER: She doesn't have to say anything, does she? It's not for her to say who our friends are, is it? I mean, we've got to keep *some* independence.

MOTHER: I'd hate not to see him again.

FATHER: Exactly. Poor old Simon . . . We'll do that, then. Good. Now let's have a go at the Bach, shall we? You know, I don't really believe in this generation gap nonsense.

THE END